W9-BNQ-406

CAMPAIGNING
FOR
PRESIDENT

CAMPAIGNING

FOR

PRESIDENT

JORDAN M. WRIGHT

Smithsonian Books Collins

An Imprint of HarperCollinsPublishers

CAMPAIGNING FOR PRESIDENT. Copyright © 2008 by Jordan M. Wright. All rights reserved. Printed in China. No part of this book may be used or reproduced in any manner whatsoever without written permission except in the case of brief quotations embodied in critical articles and reviews. For information address HarperCollins Publishers, 10 East 53rd Street, NY 10022.

HarperCollins books may be purchased for educational, business, or sales promotional use. For information please write: Special Markets Department, HarperCollins Publishers, 10 East 53rd Street, New York, NY 10022.

Object photography by Gary Mamay © 2007 by the Museum of Democracy.

All contemporary photographs by Joseph Sohm © Joseph Sohm, VisionsofAmerica.com.

All rights reserved.

First Smithsonian Books edition published 2008.

Designed by Laura Lindgren.

The Library of Congress Cataloging-in-Publication Data has been applied for.
ISBN: 978-0-06-123395-1

08 09 10 11 12   ID/TOP   10 9 8 7 6 5 4 3 2 1

For my parents, Martin and Faith Wright, who even with their sometimes limited interest in politics, always encouraged my passion for political memorabilia as a record of our nation's great democracy.

And for my children, Austin and Mackenzie Wright, to study—as history really does repeat itself—and to involve themselves in campaigns and elections which truly do affect their world and their place in it.

CONTENTS

1896–1916

1920–1948

1952–PRESENT

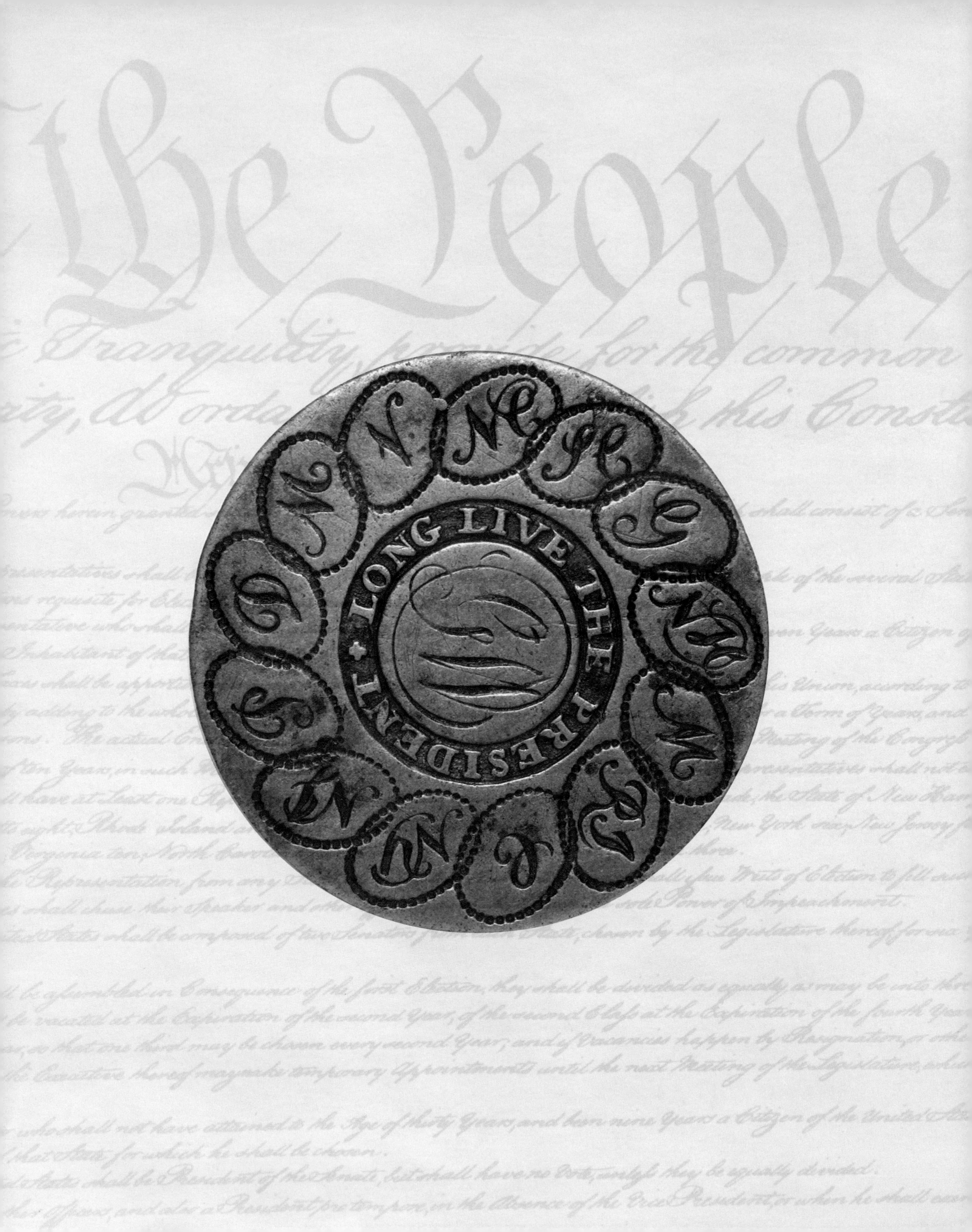
LONG LIVE THE PRESIDENT

PREFACE

It All Started with a Button

Presidential political memorabilia began with the first president of the United States. Brass clothing buttons commemorating Washington's ascension to the presidency were mass-produced. The chain of thirteen links represents the original states. Many appeared with the slogan "Long Live the President."

When I was ten, after school and before going home, I would stop off at the Robert F. Kennedy for President headquarters. It was the first place I had ever visited where people were talking about the important issues of the day, civil rights, the environment, and the war in Vietnam. As an added bonus, every week there were new buttons that you could have for free. I never missed a week. Once I got to meet Senator Kennedy. It was probably only a minute that he spent with me, but what an important minute that was! He told me how proud he was to see someone as young as I was helping to make him president. I think if Kennedy had been elected in 1968, the fate of the United States would have been very different—considerably improved.

It did not take me long to figure out that if they were giving away free buttons at the Kennedy headquarters, then they probably were at McCarthy's, Humphrey's and Nixon's presidential headquarters, too. There were, of course, also posters, bumper stickers, and campaign brochures. I collected everything I could get my hands on.

My next conclusion was that buttons and other political memorabilia could not just have been invented for the 1968 campaign. There had to be prior campaigns that produced this material; the question was how to find it.

There really is no one answer.

I found a one-of-a-kind Washington picture flag at a junk store while attending Columbia College in the 1970s. At that time, the area north of Times Square on Eighth and Ninth Avenues was overrun with peculiar and cluttered junk stores. My favorite was owned by a bickering old couple. "The kid wants to see the political stuff, where did you put it?" "I never touched it. That's your responsibility." "It is not." As they argued, I filtered through the junk, and on one visit, I unearthed the Washington flag from beneath a stack of Horatio Alger books. At first they wanted $200 for it, but I convinced them that I could barely afford one hundred. They accepted and I dashed out with the new highlight of my collection. I recently showed this picture flag to some American history buffs. One woman leaned in close to me and whispered, "Jordan, there is a rip in the corner," to which I replied, "I will call headquarters in the morning to complain and ask for a replacement." What I felt like saying was, "I hope you look as good when you are two hundred and thirty years old."

I used to work quite often in upstate New York, around the Finger Lakes. Occasionally I would treat myself to dinner at a local hotel. One evening, after dinner, I noticed swarms of people arriving. It was rare to see so many people anywhere in the area, but especially after dinner at this remote hotel. Following the crowd, I stumbled into a firemen's memorabilia show and sale. I had visited many antique shows in my life, but this was a first. There was every firefighting item you could imagine: old firemen's badges, uniforms, axes, hoses, and even ladders. I found a hand-painted leather James Monroe fireman's hat for sale, a one-of-a-kind item and a perfect addition to my collection. Apparently a local fireman who truly adored the president created the hat. I believe the sellers were descendants.

How I acquired a pro–Lewis Cass, anti–Zachary Taylor mechanical metamorphic card is truly lucky. The card shows disappointment with Taylor on one side with frowns all around, and exultation with Cass on the other. The word

Greeley wall-hanging match holder.

"Alocofoco" on the top denotes "a local folk," meaning the man portrayed is an average-Joe voter. I had purchased a framed political flag and was transferring it to another frame years later when this card fell out from behind.

Every once in a while, I get an unexpected call from someone who has heard of my collection and me. Once an elderly woman called. Her great grandmother had created a one-of-a-kind folk-art portrait of Abraham Lincoln from seeds and saplings. I had a lot of trouble guessing what this would look like, but she agreed to send it to me on approval. When it arrived, it was love at first sight. It is an extraordinary item for which I am grateful; no one in her family wanted it. At another point I got a call from someone who described himself as a descendant of "Jonnie." Jonnie was a friend of William McKinley. Jonnie had a horn that he would blast when McKinley was about to speak. This was an important job, as McKinley did not leave his front porch. Without Jonnie, people would have had to wait around all day until McKinley was ready to speak.

I found a pair of Ulysses S. Grant and Horace Greeley metal wall-hanging match holders at a store on the Lower East Side of Manhattan that exclusively sold objects made of metal. Tools, pots and pans, machine parts . . . as long as they were metal. This weird retail concept survived for almost one hundred years until the store closed in the mid-1980s.

I acquired many of my Communist Party memorabilia from my great-uncle Nat (my mother's mother's brother), who was a life-long member of the Communist Party. I learned his secret at a family dinner. In 1972, my family was split down the middle between supporters of President Nixon and supporters of Senator McGovern. My father decided that everyone present had to declare his or her preference. We went around the table and each person spoke, except Uncle Nat, who kept moving around trying to avoid my father's direct questions. He should have known better . . . my father is impossible to avoid! Finally, when there was nowhere else to hide, and my father said, "It's okay, Nat, there are others here voting for McGovern," Nat responded in a loud, clear voice, "I am going to vote for Gus Hall and Angela Davis. I have voted Communist since the party was founded and I am not going to stop now." Silence. After that I spent a lot of time with my great-uncle Nat, listening to his stories about the different campaigns. He was always finding memorabilia, or telling me where I could locate posters, leaflets, buttons, and books, all of which eventually ended up in my collection. My favorite comes from one of the best years for the Communist Party, perhaps because of this poster's strong image: a muscular worker, in red. It is from 1924 and promoted the candidacies of William Z. Foster and Ben Gitlow.

Today, my collection consists of approximately 1,250,000 pieces, beginning with the George Washington flag and five different buttons celebrating his election, as well as 4,000 items from the 2004 election; an enormous quantity of pins, posters, flags, and three-dimensional objects used in every national political campaign in United States history; ballot boxes, canes, hats, and tiles; liquor bottles and food products (such as the 1952 corn flakes box picturing Ike and Stevenson); paper and metal torches, matchbooks, umbrellas, dolls, china, license plates, LPs, commercials, and Web sites. I have not limited myself to major party nominees; I have hopefuls, third-party candidates, also-rans, and what I call pre-presidential material, such as a poster of William McKinley running for governor of Ohio. In addition, I have what I believe are near-complete collections (some composed of only one button) of every African-American, Jewish-American, Asian-American, and outed-gay candidate for the House, the Senate, or governor. My collection of female candidates for governor and senator is near-complete. The congressional collection is weaker because I refuse to collect items from men who died before they could serve in Congress—even if their widows replaced them. I am only interested in items from the women's own election or service. I have collections from cabinet members who ran for office, as well as something from each member of both Nixon's and Clinton's impeachment committees. I also have collected items from business leaders who ran for office, such as Lee Iacocca, Pete duPont, Malcolm Forbes, and J. W. Marriott.

In the last six to seven years, I have been captivated by the fact that democracy is growing overseas and, more important, that elections are organized—for better or worse—on a sort of U.S. model, with pins, stickers, pamphlets, posters, and three-dimensional objects being produced and given away to political supporters.

And finally, as a lifelong New Yorker, I collect everything that is New York: the mayors, governors, senators, Tammany Hall, gentrification, parks, holidays, the Empire State Building, the Statue of Liberty, the World Trade Center, and, of course, 9/11.

I am not quite sure what the mission of the collection is. I like collecting, and even more, I like researching who these characters from the past were. At this point in my life, I also feel a bit selfish: Unless you know me, you cannot see the collection. And therefore, I have founded The Museum of Democracy. Once it finds a permanent home, it will allow many more people to see the collection. The Museum of Democracy will not be a stale assortment of arcane campaign buttons but a living, breathing history of the democratic traditions on which we can continue to build.

Feel Good Soap encouraged voting as well as proper hygiene.

INTRODUCTION

Elections pass. During the campaign, candidates race around the nation shouting from soapboxes, doling out buttons and flyers, and basking in confetti showers at party conventions, pausing only momentarily to smile genteelly for exploding flashbulbs. But once the country crowns a winner, the enormous janitor of time picks up a gigantic push-broom and sweeps each specially crafted candidate-touting knickknack into a colossal red, white, and blue rubbish pile. Who needs a George Bush "Republican Integrity" button or a gaudy Grover Cleveland banner once the votes are tallied? Together, however, all these textiles, ceramics, lapel pieces, postcards, sheet music, posters, clothing, hats, uniforms, parade lanterns, canes, torches, games, stickers, jewelry, and license plates (to merely scratch the surface) provide tangible insight into how and why our leaders became our leaders. These gentlemen owe their presidencies in part to their memorabilia, which provided them a venue for mudslinging, created a mass dash for campaign capital, and at some points, served as the only way for candidates to communicate with their constituents. En route to the presidency, potential commanders-in-chief have stumbled and clawed and fibbed to woo the sometimes incredulous, sometimes oblivious hearts of a perpetually evolving voting public, attempting to stick their pin on every vacant lapel.

Originally, political memorabilia was a candidate's lone method of drumming up support. Before we went to bed every night with visions of the Internet and the accosting 24-hour news media dancing in our heads, before we had the opportunity to gather information in order to develop an informed opinion on a candidate (which most people still fail to do), and before the average voter could even read, how did anyone win votes? The same way that fast-food chains cajole us into buying greasy food we don't need: by pouring in heaps of money, bashing the competition, and oohaah-ing us with flashy in-the-face colors.

Let's use Joe the farmer, living in the middle of Kentucky in 1840, as our example. Other than his wife and cows, he has contact with a limited number of living things. He can't read a lick and has no way of knowing the names of the candidates, let alone forming an opinion about them. But if William Harrison holds a parade with swanky lanterns in the nearest trail-dust town and Martin Van Buren does not, which one will win Joe's vote? Or if Joe hears from a friend that courageous Tippecanoe grew up in a log cabin just like Joe did? Publicity. Marketing. The art of the smoke screen is easy when no one knows you're allowed to question.

As the years progressed, a memorabilia arms race of sorts developed, with parties violently competing to debut the newest and nicest objects. But you can't commission a masterpiece without the essential building block: money. Steadily flowing cash is old hat in the presidential race. Many men before Nixon have snuck illicit dollars, and in turn, many men before John McCain have trumpeted campaign reform. Even infallible George Washington achieved his status partly because he happened to be one of the largest landowners and richest men in the infant nation. It's silly to suggest that the war hero would not have been elected without his fortune, but the wealth certainly didn't hurt. One of the William Jennings Bryan items from 1896 was a mechanical bicycle with pictures of Republican presidential and vice presidential candidates William McKinley and Garrett Hobart on the wheels—but with their campaign manager Mark Hanna pedaling, indicating who was truly in control. Hanna raised unprecedented funds for McKinley by making outlandish promises, including allowing any big donor unlimited audiences with the president-elect, even without an appointment. Bryan's campaign items also took on trusts, likening the behemoth business interest groups to an overbearing octopus in one poster, sticking its tentacles where they didn't belong.

However, money alone cannot buy an election. You also need to bite your opponents' flesh and give it a good ole

Flipping over this one-of-a-kind doll of William McKinley reveals an African-American baby, offering an answer to the scandalous question whether McKinley fathered a child out of wedlock.

jolly rip. What race would be complete without finger-pointing, buck-passing, and an alleged scandal or two? After a few early elections of competitors repressing their abhorrence and pretending to purr around one another, candidates let the fur fly and haven't let up since. Andrew Jackson's opponents referred to him as "King Andrew the First," mocking his totalitarian tendencies, and created broadsides displaying coffins in reference to the supposedly extensive list of people General Jackson unjustly slaughtered. In 1896, William McKinley's Democratic enemies produced a very revealing doll. The fine china object features McKinley wearing an American flag in place of pants. Innocent and patriotic, right? But flipping William over and pulling the flag over his head exposes an African-American baby girl wearing a red flower-patterned dress, answering the question whether or not William McKinley had a child with someone other than Mrs. McKinley. The McKinley campaign battled back, poking fun at William Jennings Bryan's penchant for nap-inducing speeches with small coffins containing fake bodies inscribed with the lampooning phrase "Talked to Death." In 1928, Herbert Hoover's campaign produced buttons reading "A Christian in the White House," jabbing at his opponent Alfred Smith's Catholic beliefs. The 1960 Nixon campaign belittled John Kennedy's youth with "Don't Send a Boy, Send a Man" buttons. In 2000, Democrats produced postcards with the headline, "Like Father, Like Son," showing George W. Bush snuggled in his father's lap.

All the objects you'll see on the pages following are from my personal collection, which now belongs to the Museum of Democracy. Because no one can own everything, there will be gaps from time to time, where the items no longer exist or some other collector beat me to the punch. I have not listed the size and worth of each item, tedious details of little interest to noncollectors. Most of the buttons are actual size, but other objects may appear smaller or larger than in reality.

Time may skew opinions of candidates or elections, but the items don't deceive. They are uncompromising and unchangeable. They expose candidates' wrinkles, eccentricities, insecurities, cash flow, dark secrets, troublesome platforms, and anything else you care to seek out. Every four years for over two centuries, candidates have paved the road to the U.S. presidency in their own personal odd liaisons and seedy smoking room bargains, and each victor has staggered into that White House on the tattered wings and battered wheels of slogans, pamphlets, and toothbrushes bearing his name. Does that make these trinkets still valuable, now that the losers have gone home and the taste of victory on the lips of the winners has long since vanished? I'd say so.

An anti-Republican door hanger, referencing the Teapot Dome scandal.

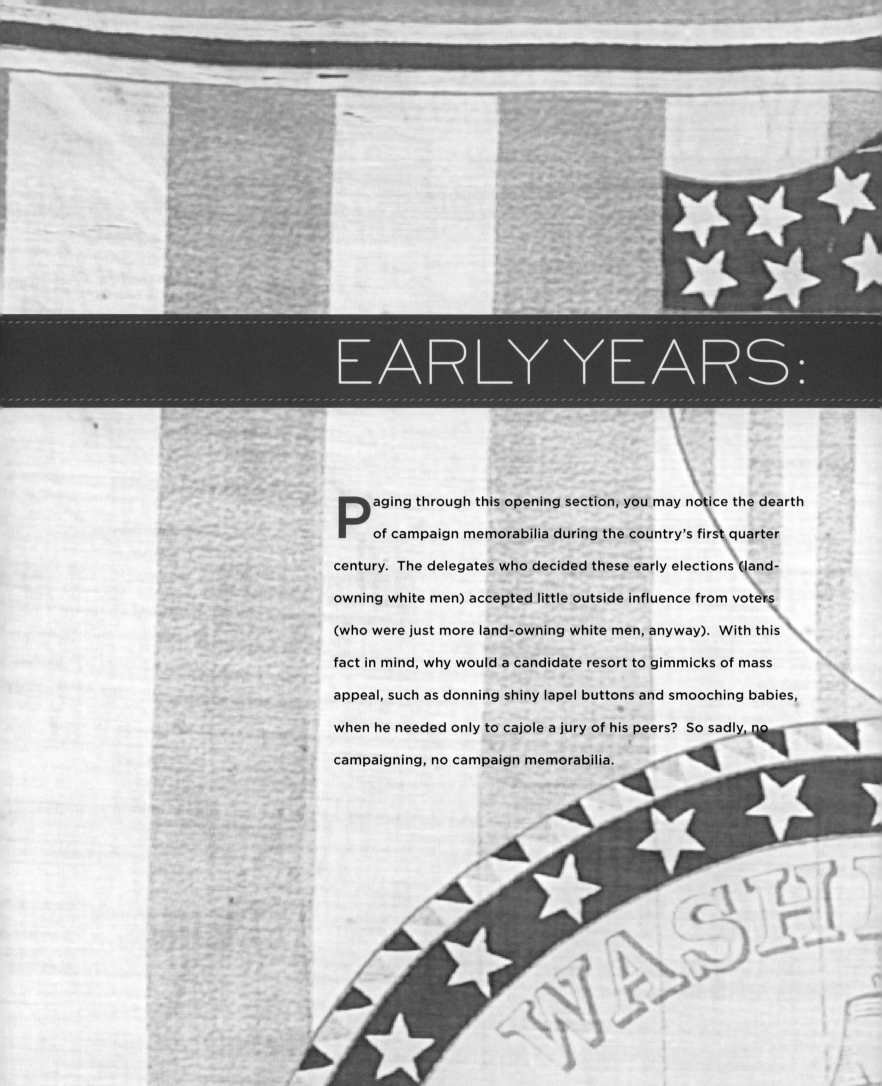

EARLY YEARS:

Paging through this opening section, you may notice the dearth of campaign memorabilia during the country's first quarter century. The delegates who decided these early elections (land-owning white men) accepted little outside influence from voters (who were just more land-owning white men, anyway). With this fact in mind, why would a candidate resort to gimmicks of mass appeal, such as donning shiny lapel buttons and smooching babies, when he needed only to cajole a jury of his peers? So sadly, no campaigning, no campaign memorabilia.

1789–1824

What does remain from the era are showy decoratives from lavish inaugurations. Brass and copper tokens created for George Washington's ceremony inspired many later campaign items, as did the "backname" buttons of James Monroe and the fancy china made for John Adams. And though smear campaigns were still years away, the Federalist/Democratic-Republican party war foreshadowed looming vicious rivalries.

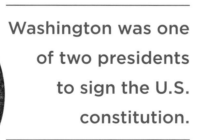

> **Washington was one of two presidents to sign the U.S. constitution.**

Spearheading the Continental Army to miraculous victory in the American Revolution gave George Washington the aura of a hero without equal. Luckily for the young republic, he had no intention of turning his reputation into absolute power. So with the level-headed Washington as the only real candidate, the biggest question in the first presidential election was not who would be president, but whether or not the newborn electoral system would work.

The delegates to the constitutional convention agreed that the country needed an effective executive, but they feared the abuses and dangers of royal or imperial power, which had sealed the fate of Rome's republic. The delegates compromised on a system of presidential electors. They assumed that electors would be property-owning white men in the states they served, and that they would have the knowledge to cast intelligent votes (women, other races, and young people were not considered). Even a system based on electors was controversial, however, because the idea of allotting electors to states simply on the basis of population encountered many of the same objections as a system of direct popular election. Solution: The number of electors from each state would equal the number of senators and representatives, thus ensuring that all states as well as populations would be represented in the election of the president.

The concern that most electors would simply vote for men from their own states was dealt with by the stipulation that one of each elector's two votes must be cast for someone outside his own state.

Under these guidelines, the electoral college met in 1789 and again in 1792, and both times, not a single elector cast a vote against Washington. He is the only president elected unanimously—twice. According to the new system, the person with the second highest electoral vote became vice president, who in both 1789 and 1792 was John Adams. His strenuous new tasks included breaking tied votes in the Senate and taking over the presidency if the president should resign or die. Adams called the job "the most insignificant office that ever the invention of man contrived or his imagination conceived."

American presidential memorabilia kicked off with the fashioning of metal garment buttons for GW's inauguration. They bore legends such as "Long Live the President" and "March the 4th 1789 Memorable Era." (Memorable Era? As you can see, we had a long way to go.) One design featured the initials GW surrounded by chains of thirteen oval links encircling abbreviations of the original states, which Washington sported when he took the oath of office.

The Washington picture flag is unique. It was used to celebrate our first president's swearing in.

Many of these early objects were the ancestors of later presidential campaign items. Small brass and copper tokens similar in manufacture and design to Washington's would become the most ubiquitous of nineteenth-century campaign items, while Washington's portrayal in uniform on various tokens and china would be repeated for future soldier-statesmen Andrew Jackson, William Henry Harrison, and Zachary Taylor.

OPPOSITE: These buttons were designed to commemorate President Washington's inauguration, including a chain of thirteen links representing the original states. Washington liked them so much that he purchased a set for himself and had the buttons sewn onto the jacket he wore during the ceremony.

Metal parade torch for John Adams. A lighted candle burned inside this unique item, illuminating Adams's name and the number one.

Adams was the first president to live in the White House.

Some political factions in the country were pro-British, others open partisans of the new republic of France. Metal tokens satirizing political events had been in vogue in England for some time. Now, for such political effect as they might create, a limited number were imported to this country. Some portray Thomas Paine—an ally of John Adams and at the time a refugee in France—hanging from a scaffold.

Washington's stepping aside to retire to Mount Vernon led to the first real presidential race and the formation of the forever-feuding factions known as political parties. In one corner sat the stuffy Federalists, with vice president John Adams at the helm, supporting a strong centralized government and life terms for senators. In the other corner, the more freewheeling Democratic-Republicans, spearheaded by former secretary of state Thomas Jefferson, favored more power for the states and limited terms in public office. The Democratic-Republicans had veiled their displeasure long enough out of respect for President Washington, but with his departure, the pot finally boiled over. The cordial comradeship Adams and Jefferson had enjoyed during the American Revolution quickly dissipated into fierce rivalry.

Washington's endorsement secured victory for Adams, but Jefferson came in second, becoming Adams's vice president, the only time in American history that the president and vice president were members of opposing political parties (making for some tense private dinners, I'm sure).

These sections include mostly inauguration items as opposed to campaign items, because at this point, there were no real campaigns. Because a small, stubborn group of politicians chose the next president without taking the popular vote into account, there was no reason for candidates to strive for mass appeal.

John Adams's inauguration memorabilia included china pitchers with his picture, and a button featuring a stylishly bewigged Adams, referring to him with the hip nickname, "Jo."

A glass-on-glass portrait of John Adams.

Sculpture of Thomas Jefferson,
Washington, D.C.

Working under the same roof for four years didn't help relations between Adams and Jefferson, and they matched wits again in 1800. Early American etiquette forbade the candidates from openly attacking each other and making public appearances and speeches on their own behalf, but that didn't stop their party members from throwing some solid roundhouses. The Democratic-Republican press battered Adams, but the still-in-power Federalists issued the Sedition Act, unconstitutionally prohibiting badmouthing Adams's administration, to squelch their competitors.

When the electoral college convened, Jefferson and Aaron Burr each received seventy-three electoral votes, defeating the Federalist ticket of John Adams and Charles Pinckney of South Carolina. Prior to the election, Jefferson and Burr had made a pact that Jefferson would be president, and Burr vice president. But with the vote tied, backstabbing Burr saw his opportunity to achieve the nation's highest office, and smugly shrugged off Jefferson's insistence that he back down. The tie tossed the election to the House of Representatives, where after thirty-five separate ballots, the vote remained deadlocked.

> **Jefferson's grandson was the first baby born in the White House.**

With the fledgling nation appearing weak and indecisive, Alexander Hamilton hesitantly stepped to the plate. With a strong influence on Federalist members of Congress, Hamilton had the power to break the stalemate, but faced an awkward dilemma. Hamilton and Jefferson never got along, but Hamilton found him far more trustworthy and competent than the pigheaded Burr. On the thirty-sixth ballot, Hamilton persuaded several congressmen not to vote at all, swinging the election to Jefferson, who became the third president of the United States.

To remedy the problem, Congress passed the Twelfth Amendment to the Constitution in time for the 1804 election, altering the rules of the electoral college so that the electors voted for the president and vice president separately.

Jefferson ran for reelection in 1804, but of course booted the disloyal Burr from the ticket, replacing him with New York governor George Clinton. Jefferson skated smoothly past Federalist candidate Charles Pinckney as the Federalists slid further into the growing shadow of the dominant Democratic-Republicans.

Jefferson's presidency inspired such items as an inaugural medalet, a hand-painted linen portrait banner (the only copy of which is in the Smithsonian), and a number of china pitchers.

1808 and 1812: **Mad for Madison**

Close-up of the James Madison memorial in the Library of Congress, Washington, D.C.

With the retirement of John Adams and the death of Alexander Hamilton, the bumbling Federalists were fresh out of capable leadership, and didn't even nominate a candidate, conceding defeat to the Democratic-Republican nominee, Jefferson's secretary of state and protégé, James Madison. Red-nosed Madison looked more like a sickly munchkin than a president. The party nicknamed him "Great Little Madison" due to his slight five-foot, four-inch, one-hundred-pound build. (He was even shorter than Napoleon.)

Madison continued the Democratic-Republicans' stronghold on the presidency. Between the terms of John Adams and his son, John Quincy Adams, the Democratic-Republicans held the White House for six consecutive terms, spanning twenty-four years. Scholars refer to this string of presidents as the Jefferson Dynasty because Madison and his successor James Monroe considered themselves protégés of Jefferson, or as the Virginia Monarchy because all three men came from Virginia.

In the midst of the War of 1812, Madison ran for reelection against former New York City mayor DeWitt Clinton, the nephew of George Clinton. A Democratic-Republican, Clinton ran independent of his party, and attempted to cater to every side. To those who supported the war, he promised to continue the fight. To those who opposed the war, he promised peace (now that's the kind of unabashedly two-faced politicking I like to see). In the end, neither side believed him, and Madison won the election, 128 to 89.

James Madison was the first president to wear trousers instead of knee breeches.

A china pitcher commemorated Madison's 1809 inauguration, and his 1813 inaugural medal was designed by Moritz Furst, one of the leading engravers of the period.

Unique red leather hat designed and worn by a New York City firefighter to show his support for James Monroe.

The secretary of state post acted as the on-deck circle for the Presidency. Jefferson won election following his tenure as secretary of state to Washington, Madison after serving as secretary of state to Jefferson, and now it was James Monroe's turn, following his tutelage under Madison.

The fading Federalists again failed to nominate a candidate, although with their talk of secession from the Union, they probably wouldn't have fared well anyway. The Feds did monetarily support Rufus King of New York, who had been George Washington's minister to Great Britain, but the King of the Federalists was no match for mighty Monroe in 1816.

They didn't call Monroe's first term *The Era of Good Feelings* for nothing. Peace, satisfactory relations with Britain, and the Missouri Compromise satiated most Americans. Why replace a president who had delivered so much prosperity? Because both Jefferson and Madison had served two terms in office, it was expected that Monroe would run again. And because the Democratic-Republicans were so sure that he would be reelected, they did not even bother to formally nominate him. What little remained of the Federalist Party did not offer any opposition. As a result, the presidential race of 1820 was essentially an election without a campaign.

Monroe was the last president to have served in the Revolutionary War.

When the electoral college met in December 1820, Monroe won all the electoral votes but one. New Hampshire governor William Plumer cast the single exception. Plumer reportedly voted against Monroe so that George Washington would remain the only president ever elected unanimously. According to Plumer's son, however, his father simply hated Monroe.

James Monroe's presidency inspired the first "backname" buttons (with the candidate's name or slogan on the back) to pin on clothing, as well as a red leather fireman's hat.

1824: **Like Father, Like Son**

By 1824, the Federalist Party had fizzled out completely, leaving four Democratic-Republicans to wrestle in a free-for-all brawl. Treasury Secretary William Crawford of Georgia, the early front-runner, suffered a stroke during the campaign, ending his candidacy. Secretary of State John Quincy Adams had the solid backing of New England, while Speaker of the House Henry Clay garnered support out west. Of all the contenders, only war hero Andrew Jackson of Tennessee could count on votes from every region of the country.

Eighteen twenty-four marked the first time states considered the popular vote important enough to count. Previously, state legislatures had determined electors, but this time around, most states allowed its citizens (though only adult white males) to vote. Jackson won more electoral votes than anyone else, but not a majority, which once again catapulted the election into the House of Representatives.

John Quincy Adams knew how to work the system. The shrewd Adams struck a backroom deal with House Speaker Clay: If he swung votes to Adams (away from front-runner Jackson), then Adams would make him his secretary of state. Sitting way back in third place in the race, Clay took the bait, and Adams won a narrow victory on the first ballot.

> Adams, the son of a former president, named his own son George Washington Adams.

1828-1852

Prior to 1828, there was no need to campaign. Each member of the electoral college had a firm grasp on politics and his own opinions, and no elaborate button or fancy slogan would change his mind. However, with the increasing importance of the popular vote, candidates needed to cater to the passionately religious, the ignorant and illiterate, the stuffy businessmen, the foul-mouthed sailors, the conceited lawyers, the backwoods hicks, and every other type of man.

Candidates needed strategies with which everyone could identify, and who can resist a soap opera complete with shameless smear and slander? What better way to improve your image in a voter's eye than providing eyebrow-raising gossip about your opponent? Beginning in 1828, the political parties let the mud fly. And by the next decade, politicians learned the power of the almighty catchphrase. The 1840 "Log Cabin and Hard Cider Campaign" was the first to see a candidate promoted with the raucous marketing ploys we've come to associate with presidential campaigns.

The use of campaign objects as partisan weapons gained steam during the 1828 and 1832 presidential races, and reached new heights with the fathers of excessive trinketry, the Whigs, who united around their mutual hatred of Andrew Jackson. The new party bore buttons and ribbons as arms against their rival. The Whig logo, a liberty cap upon a pole, had been used during the American Revolution, and the Whigs sought to create a parallel between America's revolutionary struggle against King George and their own battle against "King Andrew" Jackson. They topped off their exploitation of the past with portraits of George Washington, claiming him as the spiritual founding father of Whiggery.

As Andrew Jackson saw it, John Quincy Adams had cheated him out of the presidency in 1824, and revenge-minded Jackson proved quite the grudge holder. The bad blood split the Democratic-Republican Party into two camps: Jackson's Democrats versus Adams's National Republicans.

The election turned into a finger-pointing fest. Democrats hammered Adams for allegedly making a "corrupt bargain" with Clay to win the last election, while the National Republicans printed broadsides decorated with a line of coffins referencing Jackson's execution of soldiers for minor offenses during the War of 1812. Adams's supporters portrayed Jackson as a crude, uneducated bar brawler.

But while wealthy eastern businessmen may have found these traits repulsive, ordinary voters on the frontier saw the highly educated Adams as a privileged snoot.

Jackson had won the nickname "Old Hickory," a major asset for reinforcing his reputation for natural strength, on a march from Natchez to Nashville in 1813. As the story goes, amiable hero Jackson generously surrendered his horse to an ailing soldier, fashioned a hickory walking stick, and made the remainder of the journey on foot (through eight feet of snow and uphill all the way). His supporters made use of this myth by erecting hickory poles all over the country.

> **Andrew Jackson was the first president to ride a train.**

ABOVE: This brass token from 1824 was one of the first mass-produced campaign souvenirs. Most of Jackson's material celebrated his army career and his Battle of New Orleans victory.

RIGHT: French textile bearing the likenesses of former presidents. The frigate *Constitution* appears on the right.

OPPOSITE: Jackson's controversial military tactics inspired harsh negative campaigning, including this coffin broadside. Many held "Old Hickory" accountable for unnecessary carnage during the Creek War (1813–1814).

Some Account of some of the Bloody Deeds of
GEN. JACKSON.

Jacob Webb.	David Morrow.	John Harris.	Henry Lewis.	David Hunt.	Edward Lindsey.

A brief account of the Execution of the Six Militia Men.

As we may soon expect to have the official documents in relation to the Six Militia Men, arrested, tried, and put to death, under the orders of General Andrew Jackson, this may not be an improper time to give to the public some of the particulars of their execution, as we have them from "An Eye Witness," who appeals to Col. Russell, for the truth of every word he relates.

Harris was a Baptist preacher, with a large family. He had hired as a substitute for three months. This was the case with most of them. They were ignorant men, but obstinate in what they believed right, and what they had been told by their officers was right. They were all sure they could not be kept beyond three months, and they gave up their muskets, and had provisions dealt out to them, from the public stores, before they left the camp. This confirmed their convictions that they were right, and doing what was lawful.

Col. Russell commanded at the execution. He took the place in a large wagon. The military dispositions being made, Col. Russell rode up to the wagon and ordered the men to descend. Harris

MOURNFUL TRAGEDY;

Or, the death of Jacob Webb, David Morrow, John Harris, Henry Lewis, David Hunt and Edward Lindsey, six militia men—who were condemned to die, the sentence approved by Major General Jackson, and by his order the whole six shot.

**

The reader is reminded that it was on the 21st day of January, 1815, that General Jackson returned to the city of New Orleans from the battle ground. The British had abandoned the attempt and retired. The General was received with the strongest demonstrations of joy and attachment...

Poor JOHN WOODS; he was a generous hearted, noble fellow as ever lived, who had volunteered in the service of his country...

Gen. Jackson, detailing his progress among the Indians, in the course of which, men, WOMEN and CHILDREN, were indiscriminately "exterminated," their towns burnt, and their country laid waste...

On the 27th day of March, 1814, General Jackson had found at an Indian village, at the bend of the Tallapoosa, about 1000 Indians, with their squaws and children, "running about among their huts."...

FRANKLIN, Tenn. September 10, 1818.

A difference which had been for some months brewing between Gen. Jackson and myself, produced on Saturday, 4th inst. in the town of Nashville, the most outrageous affray ever witnessed in a civilized country...

THOMAS HART BENTON, Lieut. Col. Thirty-Ninth Infantry.
And now a member of the Senate of the United States.

This "backwards" gilt-brass button is plain on the front, with Jackson's name around the shank on the reverse side. What's the point of inscribing a name on the back of a button?

They also sponsored local picnics, parades, and barbecues, making Jackson's campaign the first grassroots effort in U.S. presidential history, and ultimately leading to, as Jackson put it, "a victory for the common man."

The 1828 Jackson-Adams rematch birthed the largest heap of political memorabilia yet designed, and for the first time, the parties used it to win votes. Adams's items included mirrors, redware tiles, and sewing boxes reading "Victory for Adams." Jackson's campaign produced small medals, garment buttons, ribbons, and flasks, but none were as effective as items emblazoned with Jackson in full military dress as the exulted hero of the Battle of New Orleans (the original in a trend that would help elect many former military men). Another unique aspect of AJ's campaign was groups of supporters calling themselves Hickory Clubs, who wore hickory sprigs as badges and gathered in public squares to plant hickory saplings or raise hickory poles.

Jackson and Adams's back-and-forth bickering led to an anti-Jackson broadside accusing him of multiple murders, while another assaulted him for having lived in sin with his wife Rachel prior to their marriage. One anti-Adams item accused the supposedly polite JQ of having procured young American virgins for the Tsar of Russia!

1832: **King Andrew**

Metal frog doorstop reads, "I croak for the Jackson Wagon."

Formerly, presidential candidates had been nominated by either a group of congressmen from the same party or by a state legislature, but in 1832, the Democrats invented the national party convention (which has since become a hallmark of unnecessary hoopla and a breeding ground for partisan poppycock) to renominate Andrew Jackson. The National Republicans put up Henry Clay, who panned AJ for his tyrannical actions, which led to National Republican cartoonists famously caricaturing the president as "King Andrew I," complete with a jeweled crown over his wiry hair.

Congress passed a bill in the summer of 1832 granting the Second Bank of the United States a new charter, but Jackson had vetoed the measure. Clay turned his support of the bank into a major issue, while loose cannon Jackson never tried to hide his bitter contempt for it. A temporarily bedridden AJ told his loyal aide and future vice president Martin Van Buren, "The bank, Van Buren, is trying to kill me, but I will kill it." Clay carried the North, but Jackson took home the South, West, and the election.

Henry Clay's trinkets paid homage to his "American System" agenda for national economic development, calling him "The Champion of Internal Improvs." Three varieties of gilt brass clothing buttons featured Clay decked out in an ancient Greek toga (even though few would argue that wearing a towel is not particularly distinguished).

Jackson razor sharpener with now illegible slogan, "Old Rough and Ready."

Henry Clay coin.

Jackson hair pin.

This anti-Jackson broadside compares him to King William IV of England. Notice the final line, "Shall he reign over us or shall the people rule?"

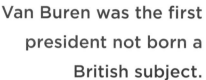

This negative broadside likens Van Buren to a horse for sale, implying that donations easily swayed his opinions.

Martin Van Buren's friendship with Jackson had won him the Democratic nomination, but also placed him squarely in the crosshairs of a steadily growing population of Jacksonian enemies known as the Whigs, who considered Jackson a pigheaded "shoot first ask questions later" cowboy. The Whigs could agree on their mutual abhorrence of Old Hickory, but not on a candidate. After much fruitless deliberation, party members decided upon the nonsensical strategy of running three candidates with regional appeal in hopes of denying Van Buren an electoral majority, which would lob the election into the Whig friendly House of Representatives: Senator Daniel Webster in the North, Hugh Lawson White of Tennessee in the South, and war hero William Henry Harrison (the only one with a viable shot at winning) in the West.

Martin Van Buren's success depended upon keeping all Democrats (northern and southern) happy, which meant avoiding the issue of slavery like the plague. Van Buren employed the "if I don't talk about the problem, it doesn't exist" philosophy and his vow of silence won him half the popular vote and a solid electoral majority.

Van Buren was the first president not born a British subject.

ABOVE: William Henry Harrison parade torch in the shape of a top hat.

RIGHT: An equestrian portrait of William Henry Harrison, surrounded by scenes of his earlier life.

OPPOSITE: The Virginia-born Houston was a key figure in the history of Texas, serving as president of the Republic of Texas, and following its assumption into the Union, as the new state's senator and later, its governor. The "Texian Grand March" (sheet music pictured here) is dedicated to Houston.

Respectfully dedicated to

GEN.ᴸ HOUSTON

and his brave Companions in Arms.

BY

EDWIN MEYRICK.

NEW YORK

Published by WILLIAM HALL & SON 239 Broadway Corner of Park Place.

Entered according to Act of Congress, in the year 1836, by Firth & Hall, in the clerks office, in the District court for the Southern District of N.Y.

1840: **Tippecanoe and Tyler Too**

With the country blaming the current economic depression on Democratic president Martin Van Buren, the Whigs spied their chance to snatch the White House for the first time. They staged extravagant events and parades with Whig trumpets blaring and Whig confetti flying, while doling out all sorts of souvenirs such as decorated hairbrushes and tobacco tins, all to promote their candidate, William Henry Harrison. Their strategy made the 1840 election, according to most historians, the first modern presidential campaign.

W.H.H.'s candidacy gained momentum when a Democratic newspaper called him a bumpkin who wanted little more than a barrel of hard (alcoholic) cider and a log cabin in which to drink it. The Whigs cleverly turned the jab into the focus of their campaign, portraying Harrison as a Jacksonian man of the people, erecting log cabins for campaign headquarters and serving hard cider in cabin-shaped mugs. They also spread rumors that Van Buren was a spoiled dandy who ate with a gold spoon and bathed in a tub of cologne. No one had to know that Harrison actually lived in a twenty-two-room mansion.

> **Harrison was the first president to die in office.**

The campaign injected such excitement into the race that an astounding 80 percent of eligible voters cast ballots. Van Buren kept the popular vote respectably close, but he lost the electoral vote by a wide margin, including his home state of New York.

In December 1839, a Van Buren–supporting newspaper, the *Baltimore Republican*, joked that a barrel of hard cider and a modest pension might induce the elderly William Henry Harrison to "sit out the remainder of his days in his log cabin by the side of a fire, and study moral philosophy." Harrison was an old man at sixty-eight, more prepared for false teeth than the campaign trail, but thanks to Whig marketing, he achieved a mythical status among frontier drunkards, with Americans clanging cider mugs together in his name at rallies, singalongs, and cabin raisings. Andrew Jackson aptly described the nonsense as "log cabin hard cider and coon humbuggery." Jackson's banners, floats, and badges featured "Old Hickory." Sadly, the Democrats failed to jump on the brassy political trinket bandwagon, producing no items in support of Van Buren.

Henry Clay clay pipe.

One of the only cloth flags produced for Harrison.

Henry Clay cotton flag banners. The "Same Old Coon" slogan references the Whigs' mascot, the raccoon.

A variety of Harrison log cabin–themed brooches and watch fobs. The gilt-glass one was imported from France.

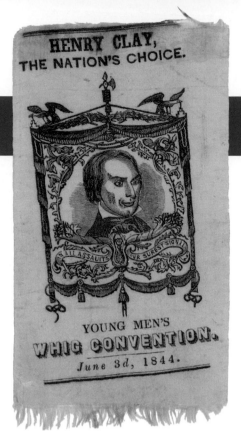

HENRY CLAY, THE NATION'S CHOICE.

ALL ASSAULTS OUR SUREST SIGN

YOUNG MEN'S WHIG CONVENTION. June 3d, 1844.

A Clay silk ribbon.

John Tyler took the presidential reins after Harrison met his Maker (after a grand total of thirty days, eleven hours, and thirty minutes in office), but by 1844, Tyler had fallen out of favor with Whig bigwigs, who opted to nominate their old friend and perennial presidential race loser, Henry Clay. Former president Van Buren racked up a majority of the delegate votes at the convention, but not the two thirds necessary for the Democratic nomination, and as the convention wore on, delegates soured on Van Buren and turned to little-known James Knox Polk, once the governor of Tennessee.

Political veteran Clay was up against a novice nobody, and he let the nation know it with the taunting "Who is Polk?" as his campaign slogan. Clay looked like a sure winner until he voiced his opposition to the annexation of Texas, which southerners interpreted as Clay trying to put the brakes on slavery. Clay lost the southern vote. He hoped his stance would win him the North, but third-party abolitionist candidate James G. Birney pointed out that Clay owned slaves. Clay lost the northern vote.

Polk saw his chance. He supported the annexation of Texas as well as Oregon as far north as latitude 54° 40' leading to the only Democratic slogan ever featuring coordinates, "Fifty-four Forty or Fight!"

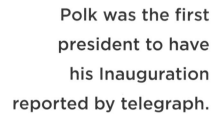

Polk was the first president to have his Inauguration reported by telegraph.

I'll tell you who Polk is, Mr. Clay. He's the next president of the United States.

Businessmen learned a lesson from the rambunctious Tippecanoe and Tyler Too campaign of 1840. The Whigs had produced a variety of items supporting Harrison and gave them to the voting public for free. Commercial vendors decided to make items for both sides and charge a small retail price. Many outlets mass-produced ribbons, ceramics, and lithograph prints, half promoting

LEFT: Coin that promoted Henry Clay's candidacy for president. Dark smoke pouring out of a factory was considered good news at the time.

RIGHT: "Free Soil, Free Speech, Free Labor" coin.

Polk-Dallas, the other Clay-Frelinghuysen. Lithographs made in factories and painted by platoons of female immigrant watercolorists were the largest selling item, and helped put a face on candidates before the advent of photography.

As far as party campaigns went, the Democratic effort for Polk exceeded its previous work for Van Buren, but couldn't begin to compete with the Whig masters. However, for the 1844 campaign, the Whigs had to tone down the ruckus and replace it with stateliness. Clay was no Log Cabin Candidate. He had camped out on Capitol Hill for decades and had inspired the "American System" and the Whig party itself. Cigar cases and ribbons ho-humly proclaimed Clay "The American Statesman," and as in 1832, many tokens and garment buttons portrayed him clad in his classical toga. One ribbon attempted to elevate him to biblical stature with a likeness of Clay on a cloudy hilltop (à la Moses on Mount Sinai) with such over-the-top maxims as "The Working Man: He Is to Society What the Main-Mast Is to the Ship." (Telegram for Mr. Clay: You're a politician, not a prophet.)

These were the first of many Grand National Banners produced by the Currier lithograph company from 1844 to 1876. A few years later, the Kellogg Company became Currier's fiercest competitor. Consumers purchased these companies' prints of presidential candidates as well as other notable historical events as collectibles.

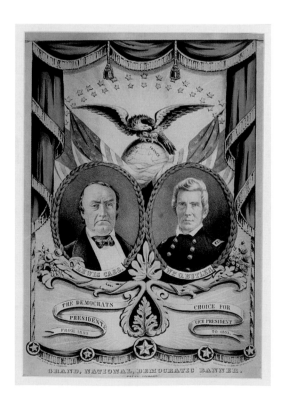

This silver stickpin advocated the expansion of slavery.

General Zachary Taylor, hero of the Mexican-American War, was perhaps the most politically apathetic presidential candidate ever. Taylor had neither run for any type of office nor even voted in an election. The Whigs courted him because of his military popularity and he begrudgingly agreed to run and accept the Whig platform, going up against the Democratic nominee, Senator Lewis Cass of Michigan.

One of the first seeds of civil war sprouted with the House of Representatives proposing the Wilmot Proviso in 1846. If passed, the bill would ban slavery in all of the territories acquired in the Mexican-American War. Cass openly opposed the measure, arguing that the citizens of each territory should be allowed to make their own decisions. Taylor refused to comment on the bill, but his sprawling plantation and ownership of more than one hundred slaves was a pretty good indication of his position.

Former president Martin Van Buren ran as the candidate of the new antislavery Free-Soil Party. Although the Free-Soilers were not yet willing to put the kibosh on slavery altogether, they opposed its spread and endorsed the Wilmot Proviso. Van Buren performed well enough in his home state of New York to swing a close election to Taylor, who won with less than half of the popular vote.

In general, the presidential elections immediately following 1844 saw an abrupt decline in political memorabilia. Parade flags, banners, transparencies, and floats are all virtually absent from the major collections of 1848 and 1852. I blame the Whigs. If you'd have stepped up your game, Whigs, then maybe your party wouldn't have folded so quickly.

This anti-Taylor mechanical metamorphic card shows either disappointment with Taylor, or if you pull the tab, exultation over Cass. The phrase "Alocofoco" on the top denotes "a local folk," meaning the man portrayed is an average-Joe voter.

OPPOSITE LEFT: A Grand National print by Currier.

OPPOSITE RIGHT: This unusual Currier print for Zachary Taylor and Millard Fillmore does not include the title "Grand National Banner" or any symbolism related to the candidates.

A Pierce clay pipe (missing its extension).

In 1852, Franklin Pierce had been happily retired from the Senate for ten relaxing years, lounging in New Hampshire. Meanwhile, in Baltimore, the Democratic convention remained deadlocked for thirty-four ballots with four candidates (Lewis Cass, William Marcy, James Buchanan, and Stephen Douglas). Desperately in need of a compromise candidate to break the tie, the Democrats displaced Pierce from his quiet home and handed him the party's

RIGHT: A colorful Currier print for Franklin Pierce.

ABOVE: A gilt-framed ambrotype (an early form of photograph), wearable as a charm.

LEFT: A gilt pendant surrounding a glass portrait of Daniel Webster.

nomination, sparking the lame slogan, "We Polked You in 1844; We'll Pierce You in 1852."

Incumbent president Millard Fillmore's endorsement of the Fugitive Slave Act alienated his northern-based antislavery party, so the Whigs nominated Mexican War hero Winfield Scott instead, known as "Old Fuss and Feathers" due to his gruff, by-the-book strictness. But with Whig infighting and such a frosty nickname, Scott never had a chance. With the backing of a united Democratic Party, Pierce took twenty-seven out of thirty-one states.

The Whigs went out with a whisper in their final official presidential campaign, with no more than three dozen known campaign objects promoting the Scott–William A. Graham effort, nearly all of which exploited the abilities of yet another (yawn) war hero. The items depicted Scott in standard military bust portraits or equestrian poses, and proclaimed him "The Hero of Lundy's Lane" and "The Hero of Many Battles." Worst of all, an overly corny bandanna read "Triumphant in war, yet the constant advocate of Peace. Ever victorious over his country's foes, his courage has only been exceeded by his humanity."

CIVIL WAR AND

With the issue of slavery bringing America to the boiling point, passion drove people to the polls in droves beginning in 1856, and in turn spurred renewed interest in campaign items. Previous standards such as brass clothing buttons as well as ceramic and glass objects fizzled, pushed out by notable new items including ferrotype disks featuring primitive photographs of the candidates in brass casings (over 160 different designs in 1860 alone) and brass badges with albumin paper photographs by 1868. For newly popular political torchlight parades, individuals would design and handpaint extraordinarily intricate paper lanterns, light a candle inside them, and march in the parade. Few survive today, for obvious reasons.

The era gave rise to a new dominant political power as well: the Republican Party. The Whigs disbanded in 1854, the Kansas-Nebraska Act ripping their free-state and proslavery wings apart

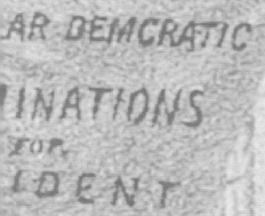

RECONSTRUCTION

Indefinitely, but their abolitionist members formed the Republicans and brought their savvy marketing campaign ideas with them. Credit a Whig for crowning Abraham Lincoln "Prince of Rails" in 1860.

However, given the ardent activism over slavery on both sides, most items focused on serious issues, especially the first Republican campaign for John C. Fremont and William L. Dayton in 1856. The Republican Party formed on the common ground of abolition, uniting the defunct Whigs with Free-Soil Party members along with other common-minded folk. In 1856, the freshly formed GOP were still awkwardly introducing themselves and reading off of each other's "Hello, my name is . . ." tags, and their regalia focused on their one common bond: antislavery. Just about all Fremont objects echoed this single-issue theme, a theme that would not go away as war loomed.

Franklin Pierce was in the doghouse. Public opinion of the president plummeted due to his weak response to growing turmoil in Kansas, and Pierce acquiesced to the masses, deciding not to run again. The Democrats needed someone disassociated from Pierce's blunders and found him in James Buchanan, Pierce's minister to Great Britain. Buchanan had been abroad for three years, he couldn't have had anything to do with Kansas, right? Buchanan believed slavery was immoral but still managed to please southern Democrats by opposing interference with already existing slavery in the South.

Battling Buchanan was John C. Fremont of California, the first candidate of the new Republican Party. Instead of allowing their dynamic nominee to naturally charm voters, the Republicans focused exclusively on abolition—a brave, bighearted stance, but not one that would win many votes. Although Fremont carried much of the North, the Democrats' broader support gave Buchanan a clear-cut victory.

A more aptly named Republican candidate would have been hard to find. The campaign items of Fremont's party banged the word "free" into voters' heads with a lead hammer. Legends included "Free Soil & Free Speech," "No More Slave States, Free Speech, Free Press, Free Labor, Fremont and Dayton," and "Free Kansas and the Union."

And Fremont was a freethinker as well as a free-soiler. The charismatic Californian could have won easily had his party not dwelt upon their abolitionist platform. Though inexperienced as a statesman, the rugged Fremont gave the Republicans a bounty of campaign options; his highly publicized exploits as a western explorer earned him the nickname "Pathfinder" and a reputation throughout the nation as a man's man in the mold of Washington and Jackson. However, the Republicans neglected to highlight any of these strengths.

> **Buchanan was the first and only bachelor president.**

FOR PRESIDENT
MILLARD FILLMORE.

MILLARD FILLMORE.
FOR VICE-PRESIDENT
ANDREW J. DONELSON.

RIGHT: A Fillmore silk ribbon.

OPPOSITE: A Grand National Banner print of the American (Know-Nothing) Party candidates, produced by Kellogg.

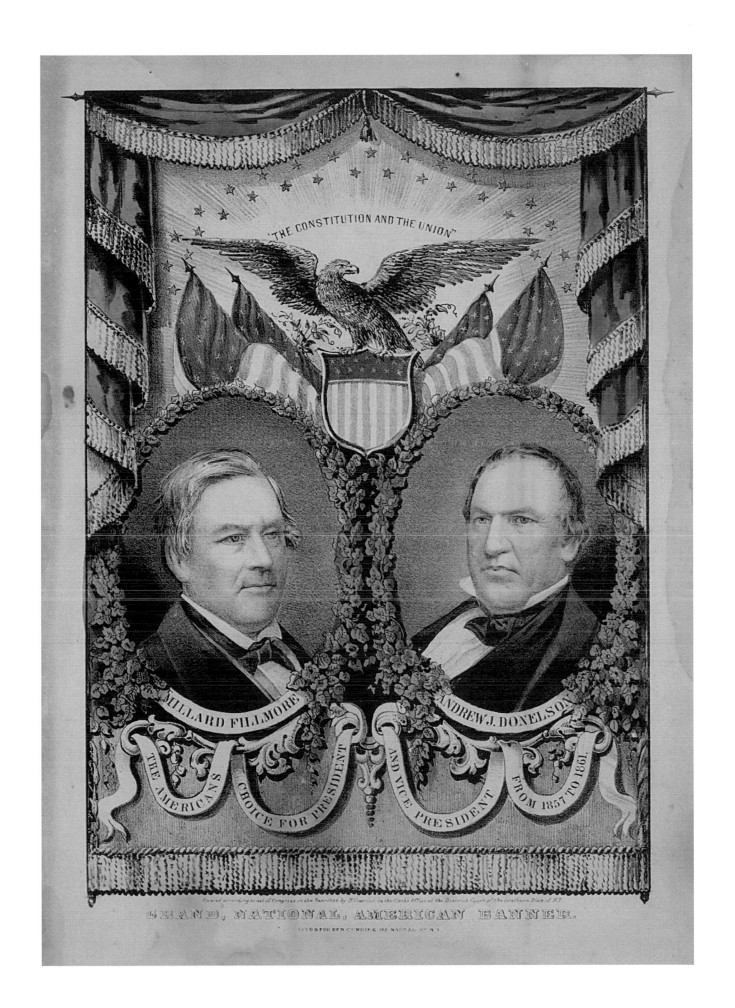

DEMOCRACY TRIUMPHANT!!!
BUCK. & BRECK. ELECTED!

The news by the train this morning confirms the glorious triumph of the National Democracy and the election of BUCHANAN & BRECKINRIDGE as President and Vice President! To prepare for celebrating this important event, there will be a

DEMOCRATIC MEETING!
AT THE
COURT HOUSE TO-NIGHT!!

Turn out, Democrats! Speeches will be made, and a Committee of Arrangements appointed to make preparations for a Torch-Light Procession, Illumination, and general Celebration of the overthrow of Sectional Know Nothing Black Republicanism! *Saturday, Nov. 8, 1856.*

PHAROS JOB OFFICE.

The Democratic campaign of James Buchanan and John C. Breckinridge diversified to a whopping two issues instead of one: proslavery and national unity. One ribbon with the caption "Black Republican" featured a running fugitive slave, and another a skull and crossbones with the legend, "Fremont and Dayton," made the Democratic position quite clear. Another ribbon portrayed fugitive slaves fleeing to Fremont's Rocky Mountains under the caption,

OPPOSITE: A Grand National Banner of the Democratic candidates by Kellogg.

ABOVE: "Buck and Breck" stands for Buchanan and Breckinridge.

BELOW RIGHT: Medal with a rebus design picturing a buck and a cannon (Buchanan).

ABOVE: Fremont ferrotype (more advanced than an ambrotype, but still not modern quality) in an ornate brass shell.

RIGHT: Fremont poster by Kellogg.

"Fremont! Free Niggers!" Southern whites fearful of threats to their property and safety donned the ribbons proudly.

More common, however, were items portraying Buchanan as the champion of national harmony. One ribbon declared, "The Union, It Must Be Preserved" with a scene portraying Buchanan and Breckinridge with Old Glory standing on the "Democratic Platform" and resting firmly upon the Constitution. A few Buchanan items with stag designs played upon his "Old Buck" nickname, and offered the Democrats' stale ongoing pun: "We Polked 'em in '44. We Pierced 'em in '52. And we'll Buck 'em in '56."

The Democrats faced stiff competition on the national unity front from ex-president Millard Fillmore, the 1856 nominee of the Know-Nothing Party. Conservative Whigs had taken over the former militant splinter group and had

given the Know-Nothings a glossy, accessible makeover. Hoping to hold Whig votes with Fillmore while appealing to Democrats with running-mate Andrew J. Donelson (Andrew Jackson's nephew), the Know-Nothings mounted a vigorous campaign centered on national solidarity, with ribbons and badges displaying Fillmore's redundant patriotic statement "I know nothing but my Country, my whole Country, and nothing but my Country" and such legends as "The Union Forever" and "National Union."

ABOVE, TOP: A cotton campaign flag with an unusual star pattern. Many flag items throughout this period rearranged the stars for aesthetic purposes.

ABOVE: A gilt frame ambrotype of John Fremont, to be worn on a chain.

A "secession" envelope styled after the Confederate flag.

John Brown's October 1859 raid on Harpers Ferry skyrocketed tensions between the North and the South, and the election of 1860 held the fate of the still-fledgling nation in the balance, the outcome determining war or reconciliation. The parties disagreed so vehemently that they released four candidates into the fray, each of whom carried at least one state in the election.

Let's meet the contestants. The Constitutional Union Party, yet another national conservative splinter group of the defunct Whigs, mobilized specifically for this election, nominating John Bell of Tennessee. Slavery position: Whatever the Constitution says, goes. Don't change a thing.

Meeting in Charleston, South Carolina, the governing Democratic Party split when front-runner Stephen Douglas refused to include a proslavery plank in the party platform. Two months later, the southern wing of the Democratic Party held its own convention, nominating current vice president John C. Breckinridge. Slavery position: vehemently proslavery, pushing congressional slave code for the territories. The northern Democrats stuck by Douglas. Slavery position: pro-Popular Sovereignty (states individually determine their slave or free status).

Lincoln was the tallest president, standing six foot, four inches.

The Republicans surprised everyone by selecting Abraham Lincoln of Illinois as their nominee. Lincoln had been out of public office for more than a decade, but all factions of the party liked him and he hailed from a critical state, Illinois. Slavery position: objected to expansion, but willing to tolerate slavery where it already existed.

Even so, the prospect of a Republican president so angered southerners that they threatened to leave the Union if Lincoln won. Lincoln and Douglas duked it out up north, while Breckinridge tried to break Bell down south. When the votes were finally counted, Lincoln won the presidency with nearly two thirds of the electoral vote but only 40 percent of the popular vote and not a single vote from the nine southern states.

With four candidates and the highest stakes in American history, everyone wanted to be involved. Each candidate organized a grassroots campaign, an army of volunteers with peculiar names such as Lincoln's Wide-Awakes and Rail Splitters, Douglas's Little Giants, Little Dougs, and Chloroformers (cleverly dubbed for its boast to "put the Wide-Awakes to sleep"), Breckinridge's National Democratic Volunteers, and Bell's Union Sentinels and Bell Ringers. Altogether their ranks numbered nearly a million, more than one for every five votes cast. These corps staged an exorbitant number of public events, most notably spectacular torchlight parades, which were witnessed by millions.

The Republicans brought out their A-game in 1860. No longer were they the

OPPOSITE: Enormous print of Lincoln in gilt frame.

Ferrotypes for the four major candidates.

one-issue chumps of 1856. Their campaign drew upon the politics of personality and symbolism, and when Lincoln's objects did focus on issues, they were highly organized and reflected regional priorities. The campaign marketed Lincoln to just about every demographic, and is viewed as one of the most effective in history.

The Republicans' plan was to paint Lincoln as an average Joe, someone that anyone would trust. They christened Lincoln with a nickname chockfull of down-to-earth homespun integrity that people still use today: "Honest Abe." And if "Honest Abe" was his name, rail splitting was his game. Longtime Lincoln chum Richard Oglesby came up with his friend's dominant symbol, the

split rail, which remarkably summed up the epic notions of Lincoln's heroic rise from humble origins, the mystique of the frontier, and the dignity of free labor into an easily marketable package. Lincoln's Wide-Awakes toted real rails in their parades, as well as wooden axes engraved with the legends "Old Abe" and "Prince of Rails." The final element in Abe's image was his western background, critical not only to court his region, but to play on easterners' enduring

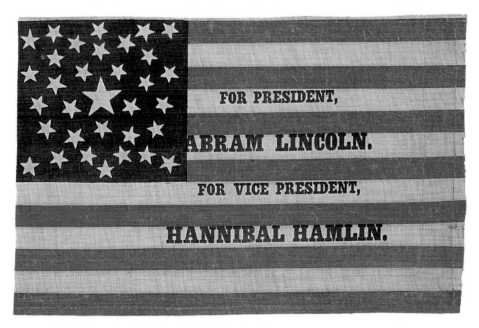

When Lincoln was nominated, many Easterners did not know how to spell his first name, as demonstrated on this cloth flag.

Abraham Lincoln Toni Kin
or
Æsop Towoyake Kin.

ABOVE: James Garvie wrote a biography of Abraham Lincoln and translated it and *Aesop's Fables* into the Santee Sioux language for use in the tribe's schools.

FOR PRESIDENT,

JOHN BELL.

FOR VICE PRESIDENT,

EDWARD EVERETT.

The Union and the Constitution.

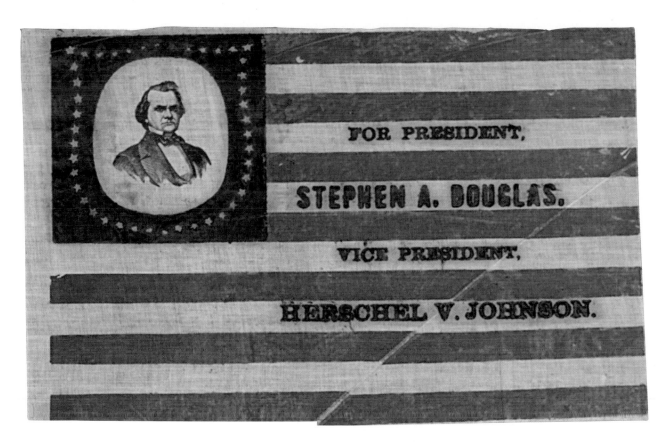

fascination with the Wild West. "Honest Abe of the West" was a popular tune of the time, and tokens bore the matter-of-fact plea "The Great Rail Splitter of the West Must and Shall Be Our Next President."

The three opposing candidate camps claimed that the Republicans' steadfast stances on slavery and other issues made them a disruptive force threatening the Union. The Lincoln camp combated the accusations with tokens, banners, and ferrotypes proclaiming "The Union Must and Shall Be Preserved," igniting an "I love the Union more," "No, *I* love the Union more" battle among all four candidates.

John Bell didn't belong to the Constitutional Union Party for nothing. Aside from a few clever campaign objects picturing a bell, all his items centered on one word looped endlessly . . . Union . . . Union . . . Union. Tokens urged "The Constitution and the Union/Now and Forever," "Union Forever/Freedom to All," and "Constitution and Union."

Stephen Douglas was a devout Unionist as well, but he approached the theme through his theory of popular sovereignty, with tokens warning "Intervention Is Disunion 1860/M.Y.O.B." (standing for "Mind Your Own Business") and crowning Douglas "The Champion of Popular Sovereignty."

The southern Democrat John C. Breckinridge put forth the least effort in the "I love the Union" fest, opting mostly to campaign for southern rights, with tokens reading "Our Country and Our Rights." The southern Democratic campaign's defiant unwillingness to compromise led to a token urging "No Submission to the North," which the party later paired with a reverse of another Breckinridge token celebrating "The Wealth of the South/Rice Tobacco Sugar Cotton" to make a very popular memento for Confederate enthusiasts.

Metal ballot box from Ohio used during the 1860 election.

Ornate Lincoln *carte de visite* (precursor to the postcard) with a gilt frame portrait.

With the Union army ensconced in a bloody, seemingly endless uphill battle, beleaguered Lincoln had to somehow find the time for a reelection bid. He ran in 1864 as the candidate of the Union Party, a zippy temporary name change adopted by Republicans to include southern Democrats still loyal to the Union. Emphasizing this political marriage, Lincoln swapped Vice President Hannibal Hamlin with southern Democrat Andrew Johnson, the military governor of Tennessee.

The northern Democrats nominated George B. McClellan, whom the president had dismissed as commander of the Union army two years earlier. McClellan pointed the finger at Lincoln for the poor performance of Union troops and called for both an immediate cease-fire and a negotiated peace treaty with the South.

During July and August, with the Union Army struggling feebly, McClellan appeared to be leading the race. However, Sherman's capture of Atlanta in

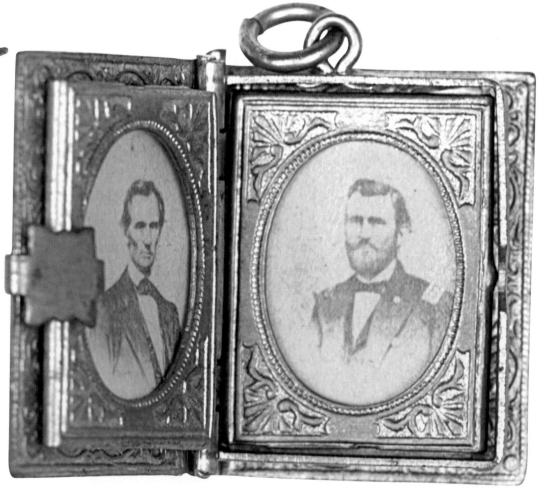

ABOVE: Lincoln cardboard badge with photograph.

RIGHT: A campaign locket with photographs of Lincoln and Grant.

Head-Quarters Nineteenth Ward Union Lincoln
Campaign Club.

THE SHIP OF STATE.

For three years the Ship of State has encountered a storm more terrific than the world ever witnessed.

During all this time, amid lightnings and hurricane blasts, the Pilot,

ABRAHAM LINCOLN,

With an honest and true heart, a courage unawed, because of a firm reliance on an overruling Providence, with steady nerves and clear eye, has stood at the helm!

Now the storm is breaking away! The port, a haven of safety, is in full view! It soon will be reached, and hosannas will soon ascend to God for a Nation's preservation!

Are there any so base as to endeavor to scuttle the Ship, freighted as it is with the fondest hopes of so many millions of the present and of the future?

Are there any conspirators who would throw overboard the brave old storm-beaten **PILOT**, who has so nobly done his duty?

If there be any such, let them come into the light of day, and not skulk into the dark corners of the hold of the vessel.

☞ Come forward, Citizens of the Nineteenth, and join the Union Lincoln Campaign Club, which meets every Tuesday Evening at Dingledein's, 3d Ave., between 59th and 60th Sts., and let us sustain our faithful PILOT.

J. F. ZEBLEY, President.

N. S. HUESTED, Secretary,

New York, March 1, 1864.

A Lincoln campaign headquarters poster.

Independent publishers printed biographies such as the one pictured and sold them to the literate public.

This one-of-a-kind folk art portrait of
Lincoln is made from seeds and saplings.

ABOVE: These hand-painted paper lanterns are leftovers from torchlight parades. Candles lit inside the lanterns would burn them completely by evening's end.

OPPOSITE: A Grand National Banner print of McClellan and Pendelton by Kellogg.

September demonstrated to the country that the war had turned. Near the end of the campaign, McClellan tried to renege his call for peace talks. The public's renewed confidence in their Abe carried him to an easy victory in November.

The war reduced campaign activity to an extent, but campaigns still turned out a hefty load of items. It was an especially fertile year for ferrotypes and tokens, leading one to wonder whether the Union could have significantly shortened the war had they used the metal to make artillery rather than trinketry.

GRAND NATIONAL DEMOCRATIC BANNER.

PEACE! UNION! AND VICTORY!

MAJ. GEN. GEORGE B. Mc CLELLAN.

LEFT: The first brooch of its kind produced for a presidential candidate.

BELOW: Ferrotype portraits of General McClellan set in ornamental brass frames.

McClellan tokens portrayed him in the trademark snoreworthy military bust style or in equestrian poses, urging "One Flag and One Union Now and Forever" and "Union and Constitution, One and Indivisible," while Lincoln's bore such similar sentiments as "Our Country and Our Flag Now and Forever" and "May the Union Flourish." The campaign of 1864 saw about 250 different types of items, just about all of which touted the Union. (I know it's wartime, but variety is the spice of life any time, gentlemen.)

T he Civil War ended the political marriage of Lincoln-Johnson's Union Party. With the greater cause won, it was high time to get back to petty bickering and pointless infighting. President Andrew Johnson returned to his old party, but didn't have a chance at the 1868 Democratic nomination after his rivals, the Radical Republicans of Congress, twice attempted to boot him from office because of his Confederate sympathies. (Impeachment does impair your ability to be reelected.) The Democratic nod went to Horatio Seymour of New York.

The Republicans chose Civil War hero Ulysses S. Grant unanimously on the first ballot. Grant's battlefield bravado helped stamp out the Confederacy; his "Let Us Have Peace" campaign slogan fit perfectly with a country tired of war and Reconstruction.

The election hinged on the parties' opposing plans for Reconstruction. The Republicans planned to continue the radical program they had passed over Johnson's vetoes, while the Democrats wished to coddle the South back to health. White southerners supported Seymour's plan overwhelmingly, although new laws forbade former Confederates from voting. Their former slaves could vote, however, and these freed men voted in huge numbers for Grant.

The only thing larger than Ulysses S. Grant's beard was his ego. He liked to take credit for winning the Civil War, and it showed in his campaign materials. Flags, bandannas, buttons, and pins all sported a gallant Grant

Grant was the first president to write his memoirs, which were published by Mark Twain.

I thought ties were uncomfortable, but this Grant cardboard shirt collar seems considerably worse. They were sold in different sizes and packaged in the box pictured.

A Grant boot-shaped pin.

A Grant paper lantern.

FOR PRESIDENT   FOR VICE PRESIDENT

GRANT AND COLFAX

LIBERTY AND LOYALTY

JUSTICE AND PUBLIC SAFETY

Entered according to Act of Congress in the year A.D. 1868 by Currier & Ives in the Clerks Office of the District Court of the United States for the Southern District of N.Y.

NATIONAL UNION REPUBLICAN BANNER, 1868.

PUBLISHED BY CURRIER & IVES, 152 NASSAU ST. NEW YORK.

Pendleton Escort, Cincinnati.

OPPOSITE: A Grand National Banner of President Grant and his new running mate Schuyler Colfax, by Kellogg.

ABOVE, BOTTOM: Pendleton ran as the nominee from the Greenback Party, which consisted mostly of farmers wishing to increase the amount of paper money in circulation.

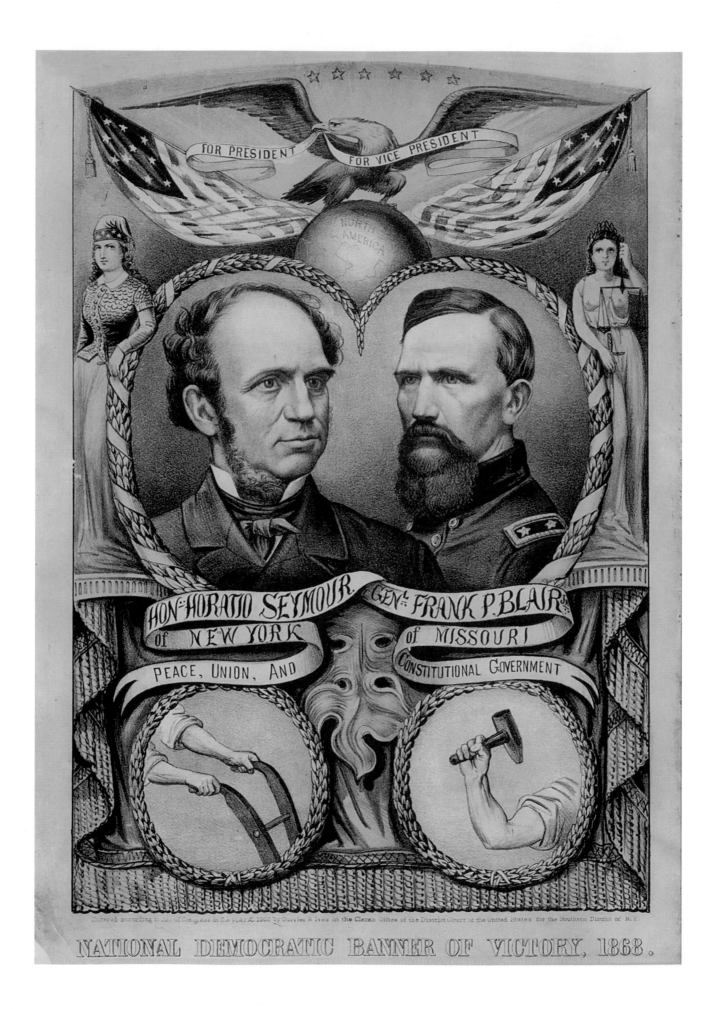

celebrating some great victory and calling himself "Freedom's Defender," "First in the Hearts of His Soldiers," and "Serene Amidst Alarms/Inflexible in Faith/Invincible in Arms."

In contrast, most 1868 Seymour items opted for Union-touting and the ever-popular pervasive racism. Medalets bore the inscriptions "Union & Constitution/Preservation of the Rights of the People" and "No North, No South/The Union Inseparable." White supremacist items included an oval brass lapel pin bluntly stating "This Is a White Man's Government," and a ribbon read "Our Motto: This Is a White Man's Country; Let White Men Rule."

OPPOSITE: This print of the Democratic candidates was meant to appeal to hardworking farmers and metalsmiths.

LEFT: Did designers realize that this pin surrounded Seymour with a Star of David?

I bought this metal and glass ballot box in New Hampshire. It's still locked. There are still ballots inside. How many other votes have remained uncounted over the years?

1872: **The Sage of Chappaqua**

Grant found himself mixed up in the wrong crowd. Upon ascending the presidency, he had infuriated party leaders by handing positions of power to inexperienced war buddies who, by 1872, made Grant look like a fool. The Republicans renominated prodigal son Ulysses despite these shortcomings, but his bashers, the liberal Republicans, tossed their convention invitations in the trash and named their own candidate, New York newspaperman Horace Greeley. The scrambling Democrats saw a seat on the Greeley bandwagon as their only chance of dethroning Grant, so they checked their pride at the door and boarded.

This beach ball–style lantern was hung at Grant's hard cider rallies, shedding light on the whiskey, music, and dancing.

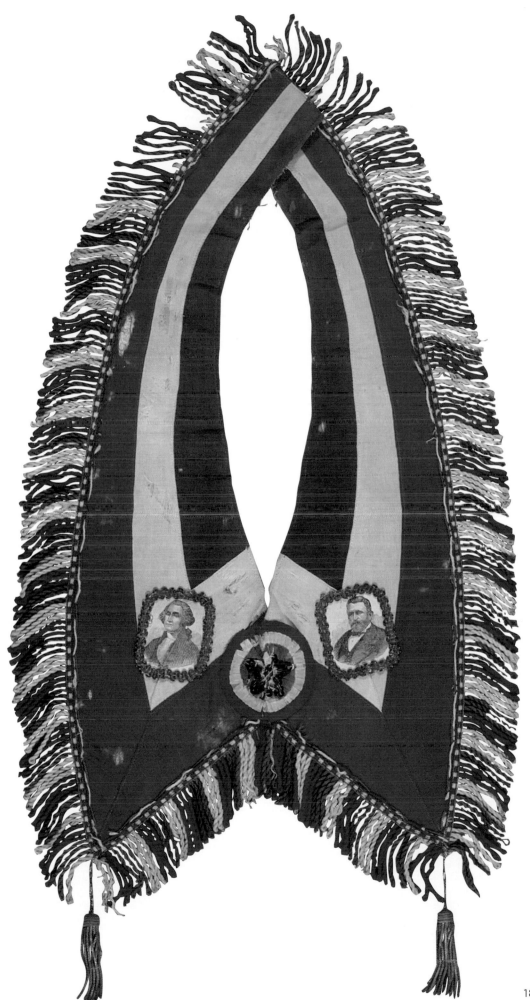

ABOVE: This portrait match safe stored matches under Grant's head.

LEFT: This piece was worn around the neck by Grant supporters during torchlight parades. I found it among the recently-out-of-style items in a northern California vintage clothing store.

ABOVE: Grant dancing toy.

BELOW: Wooden toy train with President Grant as the engineer.

OPPOSITE: A Grant glass pane to hang in a window. What do the nude cherubs have to do with Grant?

Greeley had made a name for himself at the *New York Tribune* by championing the working man and denouncing big business in his popular editorials, but he lacked Grant's focus and universal appeal. And with Greeley inexplicably taking the high ground, letting the Grant administration scandals lie (Why, Greeley? The first lesson in politician school is to kick a dog while he's down), the president's backers persuaded voters that Grant was a victim and not responsible for the corruption. The result was a resounding victory for Grant. Shortly after Election Day, Greeley grew increasingly distraught over his imminent loss to Grant, his wife's death, and his waning hold on the *Tribune*, plunging into a mental breakdown and his own death before the electoral vote was even counted.

Despite the steady stream of embarrassing scandals Grant carried with him as a first-term legacy, the Republicans still presented Grant as a military hero on his regalia, which included hand-blown crystal goblets and banners. His overwhelming reelection over Horace Greeley created a few unique items including little ivory telescopes and iron match sets, featuring the candidates'

GRANT

ABOVE: On this pin, Greeley's whiskers are made from human hair.

BELOW: A Greeley portrait fan distributed at the Democratic convention. On the reverse side is a cartoon history of Greeley's life.

faces, for mounting near a stove or fireplace. The matches were conveniently stored in either Grant's cap or Greeley's hat.

Greeley's contradictory campaign posed a real challenge for designers. How do you market a guy running as a Democrat with a Radical Republican background against a Republican? And strangely, the Democrats and the idealistic Republican defectors failed to exploit their only common ground: outrage over Grant's scandals. Instead, liberal Republican items tried to play on Greeley's intelligence (though he wasn't quite sharp enough to run a smart campaign), identifying him as "The Sage of Chappaqua" on numerous tokens.

1876–1892

By 1876, North-South bad blood had cooled, though temporarily. With the huge issues of slavery and secession gone, the public longed for escapism, and they found it by making politics entertaining (a huge feat, may I add). The 1876–1892 elections launched unprecedented grassroots campaigns, unusually high voter turnouts, and of course, a plethora of trinkets.

The ribbon emerged as the weapon of choice with built-in brass pins and festive reds and flashy blues replacing the drab "so early-nineteenth century" blacks and whites. Rivaling ribbons were bandannas, sparking the 1888 "Battle of the Bandannas" (in which thousands of working men used either Cleveland or Harrison bandannas to wipe their sweat-drenched brows), as well as metal pin-on badges and lapel studs. Cheaper to produce and much more ornate, these new innovations put an end to the ferrotype around 1880.

However, the real treats of the late 1800s were the head-shakingly wacky novelty items. Mechanical nose-thumbers were a tacky yet humorous way to express disdain for the opposition. Flip-up presidential chairs looked more like minitoilets than thrones. Inspired by the quip, "Would you vote for Harrison?" "Not in a pig's ass, I wouldn't!," campaigns produced risqué little pigs with pictures of Cleveland, Harrison, Winfield Scott Hancock, and other candidates visible through the anus. Other odd trinkets included inscribed horseshoe nails (to help obtain the all important horse vote), bridle rosettes featuring teeny candidate portraits, umbrellas, and razors. Campaigns and private vendors spent top dollar on all this throwaway silliness. However, the sassy tongue-in-cheek tone of all these nonsensical pieces injected some needed fun back into politics after the tumultuous Civil War era.

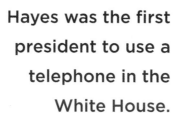

The first cufflinks produced featuring the image of a candidate (Hayes).

Hayes was the first president to use a telephone in the White House.

After eight years of Ulysses S. Grant idly turning his head while his subordinates stole everything including the rug out from under him, the country longed for a man of character. The Republican candidate, Rutherford B. Hayes of Ohio, was a known reform-minded administrator, and his Democratic opponent Samuel J. Tilden of New York, an even more famous reformer, had unsheathed his do-gooder sword on New York City's notorious Tammany Hall.

Voters made Tilden the early favorite, but the Republicans were still the stronger national party, and Hayes's own squeaky-clean reputation kept the race tight. Upon tallying the vote, Tilden appeared to have won the election, but twenty electoral votes remained in doubt, with Tilden needing just one

A Hayes paper torch.

Hayes and Tilden silk ribbons.

more to win. The disputed votes were tossed to a special election commission made up of ten congressmen and five Supreme Court justices, who voted 8 to 7 along party lines to give every last disputed vote to Hayes, giving him a 185 to 184 victory.

Tilden was cheated and southern Democrats cried out, "Oh no, you didn't," threatening to put up their dukes in retaliation to what they interpreted as the prissy northerners sneaking off with another election. But the saintly Tilden restrained them, and to save himself from the wrath of the South, Hayes agreed to the Compromise of 1877, which promised to withdraw all federal troops from the South, rebuild southern railroads destroyed during the Civil War, and

include at least one southern Democrat in his Cabinet. This backroom bargain appeased the seething South and accelerated Reconstruction.

The poorly financed goody-two-shoes contest of 1876 was predictably boring in the memorabilia department. Several items celebrated the centennial, while the rest advocated reforms, including an "Honest Money/Honest Government" Hayes token and a banner proclaiming Tilden "The Aggressive Leader of Reform." With both candidates trumpeting the same issue, it was tough to tell them apart.

ABOVE: This is a bookmark. There is a Hayes mate.

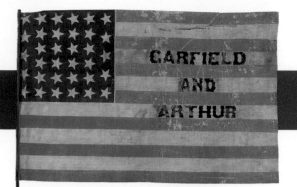

Garfield tin stickpin.

Grant for president again? President Hayes honored his promise outlined in the Compromise of 1877 by not seeking reelection, and Grant's fans persuaded him to try for a third term. Opposing him for the Republican nomination were Senator James G. Blaine of Maine and Hayes's treasury secretary, John Sherman of Ohio.

Grant held the lead at the convention for thirty-five ballots but remained about seventy votes shy of the needed total for victory. On number thirty-four, delegates cast sixteen votes for a compromise choice, Ohio congressman James Garfield, who had earlier delivered a rousing rant in Sherman's favor. Wishing to remain loyal to Sherman, Garfield hilariously jumped up in the midst of the immense hall full of bearded fifty-somethings and shouted, "I won't permit it!" Two ballots later, the Blaine and Sherman forces drafted him to keep guppy Grant out. To go against Garfield, the Democrats nominated Winfield S. Hancock, a former Union army general and military governor during Reconstruction.

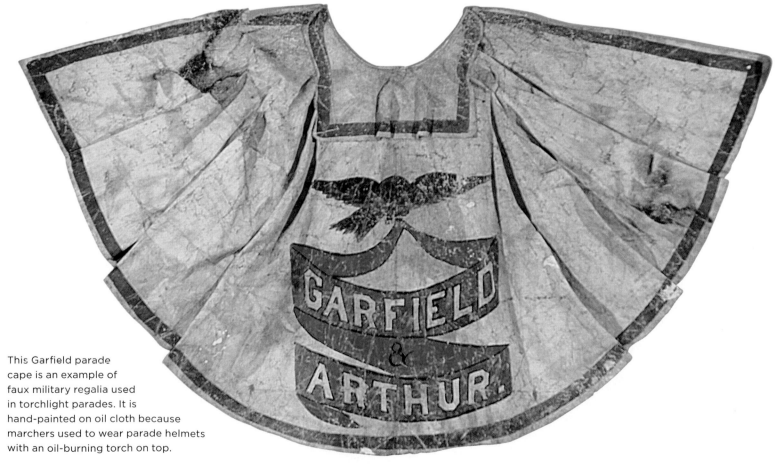

This Garfield parade cape is an example of faux military regalia used in torchlight parades. It is hand-painted on oil cloth because marchers used to wear parade helmets with an oil-burning torch on top.

Garfield and Hancock ribbons.

Lithograph tobacco tin with rotating mechanical disk that shows both presidential candidates and their running mates. Sadly, the metal-on-metal design scratches the candidates' faces each time it's rotated.

The reverse of this wooden painter's palette with Garfield's portrait is an advertisement for the Atlantic and Pacific Tea Company.

A Garfield metal oil lamp. A mystery woman is pictured on the reverse side: it is either his wife or his mother.

MY CHOICE

J. A. GARFIELD.   C. A. ARTHUR

1880

These cards were distributed to Garfield supporters at rallies.

The top of this box is made of rubber gouda, a moldable material that hardens. Boxes exist for Garfield and his vice president, Arthur (pictured), who became president when Garfield was assassinated.

GARFIELD.

COPYRIGHT

HANCOCK.

COPYRIGHT

Mechanical metal nose-thumbers (produced for Garfield and Hancock). Depressing a lever in the candidate's heel sprang the rude toy into action. These are actually two and a half inches tall.

With the race tight, clever Garfield drew up a secret agreement in the errant shadows of a Manhattan midnight with New York senator Roscoe Conkling, which is now known as the Treaty of Fifth Avenue. Garfield agreed to consult Conkling on all federal appointments made in New York, in exchange for New York's whopping thirty-five electoral votes. By a paper-thin margin (just ten thousand ballots), New York handed the election to Garfield.

Eighteen-eighty was the year of the general. With Hancock a stranger to civilian politics and Garfield compulsively eager to please everyone, both men shied from the issues, opting instead to portray themselves as every other candidate-general had before: in uniform, sometimes perched upon a trusty steed. (Didn't

LEFT: Hancock ferrotype portrait in gilt frame.

ABOVE: Hancock rebus stickpin.

anyone get fed up with the same lame military marketing year after year?)
Hancock's tokens called him "A Superb Soldier" and outlets such as Gaynor and
Fitzgerald of New Haven wholesaled the "Hancock Army Corps Pin," featuring
a cloverleaf, the symbol of the corps Hancock commanded. The Republicans
touted Garfield as a "Farmer/Scholar/ Soldier/Statesman" on bandannas, and
the items for Grant, yet another general, launched even more military busts into
the fray.

Unlike one-time-use paper lanterns, this Blaine metal and glass design could be reused in multiple parades.

The Democrats were sick and tired of losing. The Republicans had shut them out of the White House for twenty-eight straight years, but the Democrats believed they had found their savior in Governor Grover Cleveland of New York, the toppler of Tammany Hall (the society of crooks controlling Democratic politics in New York City). With President Arthur's constant flip-flopping on issues peeving too many party members, the Republicans picked James G. Blaine, who achieved nomination following two fruitless presidential attempts in 1876 and 1880.

Neither side had to dig very deep to find dirt on its opposition, especially on Mr. Blaine. First, the Democrats unearthed the Mulligan Letters, a series of documents implicating Blaine for accepting bribes from railroad higher-ups while serving in Congress. Then onlookers caught him dining with famous robber barons.

Not to be out-mudslung, the Republicans rummaged through

Blaine earned the nickname "White Plumed Knight" on the floor of the House of Representatives for talking his way out of the accusations of having accepted bribes.

LEFT AND ABOVE: Plumed knight–themed pins.

Cleveland's closet and found a nice juicy skeleton: Ten years earlier, he had fathered a son out of wedlock. But because the Democratic nominee immediately admitted the truth, most voters miraculously didn't hold it against him. To the nasty Republican chant, "Ma, Ma, where's my Pa?" the Democrats quipped, "Gone to the White House, ha, ha, ha!"

The Blaine camp was not as quick with snappy comebacks, though they desperately needed something. Just a few weeks before the election, the public interpreted Blaine's Protestant pal, Reverend Burchard's "Rum, Romanism, and Rebellion" comment as a jibe on Roman Catholics, leaving Blaine bumbling around frantically with buckets and sopping wet socks in attempts to bail out his reputation. Too late. Blaine lost the Irish Catholic vote, which lost him New York's electoral votes, which in turn cost him the election.

With the Democrats revamped, the Republicans rickety, public interest intense, and the addition of some colorful splinter-party entries, 1884 blew whistles and bells and stomped its feet like no election since the "Great Commotion" of 1840. Republican items for the flashy Jimmy Blaine hailed him as the "Plumed Knight," and odd items included the brand-new for fall (get ready, ladies), James Blaine pocketbook.

Blaine and Logan metal belt buckle.

With the Republicans doffing their tradition of bland compromise candidates, the Democrats saw 1884 as their year to pounce. For once, sufficient funds allowed them to compete with the Republicans in the memorabilia arms race. From a thematic standpoint, however, the Democratic items reflected their dull nominee. With such endearing nicknames as "Uncle Jumbo" and "His Obstinacy," the stubborn and tubby Cleveland was no Plumed Knight. To deflect attention from their candidate's persona, Democratic objects sought to exploit his reputation for integrity with such legends as "Reform" and "Public Office a Public Trust." The most disappointing aspect of the otherwise-invigorating 1884 race was the lack of personal attacks through memorabilia. Though both candidates mounted extensive verbal assaults, "Ma, Ma, Where's My Pa?" banners and the like were nowhere to be found.

Eighteen eighty-four saw the first significant volume of third-party candidacy campaign items. To me, the sheer beauty of third-party objects is they have no need to straddle issues to avert defeat, so they can be as nasty and sassy as they please. The 1884 Prohibitionist ticket of John P. St. John and William Daniel featured a lapel pin with the names of the candidates scrawled across an upside-down wine glass, but zany prizewinner was the National Greenback Labor Party

---

Cleveland was the first Democrat elected president after the Civil War.

The first campaign memorabilia shaving razor.

OPPOSITE: This 1884 poster displaying the Democratic platform hung at local campaign headquarters. Its deluge of text would have been a bit much for the mostly illiterate public.

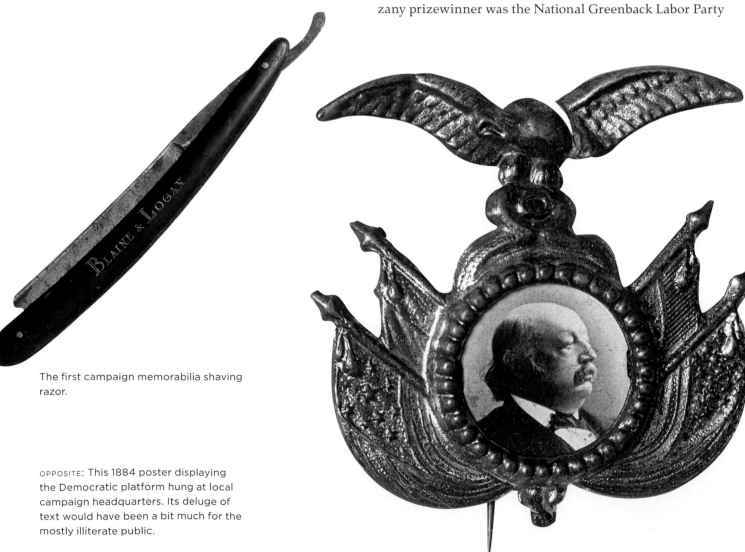

I have never figured out how to use this Blaine spinning toy. Perhaps it's missing a piece or two.

This fake dollar supported Butler's stance against the state and federal governments taking on debt.

LEFT: Cleveland rooster pin (the rooster, along with the more famous donkey, is a mascot of the Democratic Party).

candidacy of Benjamin Butler. With a penchant for unpopular causes and a face magnificently prone to caricature, his opponents made soap figures accenting his unfortunate droopy eyelid, and iron banks with his face on a frog body. But don't feel sorry for Butler, who was a singular breed: a self-deprecating politician. Pro-Butler lapel pins utilized spoon motifs, parodying his identity as "Silver Spoons Butler" for allegedly leaving his command during the Civil War with a coffin full of silver spoons. (Where were the silver forks and knives?)

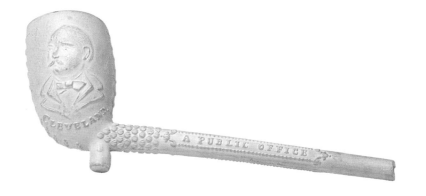

LEFT: Campaign season was a great time to start a small business. Many enterprising citizens bought campaign items in bulk (such as this Cleveland clay pipe) at wholesale prices and resold them to friends and neighbors.

Cleveland had clipped the quarter-century-plus Republican dynasty, and the seething Republicans yearned for vengeance. They chose Benjamin Harrison to front the fight. A former senator from Indiana and the grandson of president William Henry Harrison, he prompted the slogan "Grandfather's Hat Fits!" (or maybe they just had the same hat size).

Both candidates' dull homebody demeanor turned 1888 into a snoozefest (where's Blaine eating with a robber baron when you need him?). Cleveland made only one public appearance, while Harrison, per the advice of his campaign manager, stayed home in Indianapolis, and when he felt inspired, an assistant would blow a huge horn, alerting people from far and wide. Harrison would then groggily deliver a canned speech from his porch to the people assembled in front of his house.

The candidates' similar party platforms made them even more indistinguishable. Both men favored lower taxes and a larger navy, with the only real discrepancy involving tariff reform. Cleveland wanted lower rates, and the Republicans, who favored high protective rates, used this issue to bring him down.

Harrison was the first president to use electricity in the White House.

A scale with a ceramic Cleveland and Harrison suspended from wood. You can move the figures to tip the balance in your desired candidate's favor.

LEFT: Cloth covered, dangerous-looking Democratic parade helmet.

ABOVE AND BELOW: In the days leading up to the 1888 election, people used paper hat liners to avoid political arguments. Gentlemen on the street would tip their hats to each other, revealing a paper stuffed inside picturing the candidates each man supported. If one man's hat had a picture of Benjamin Harrison and the other's Grover Cleveland, they would simply steer clear of political conversation.

ABOVE AND OPPOSITE: Cleveland and
Harrison paper lanterns.

SMOKE
EL DORADO,
NOX ALL,
ROCK BOTTOM,
POR LARRANAGA
CIGARS

DEMOCRATIC NATIONAL CANDIDATES.

RIDDLE, GRAFF & CO.
MANUFACTURERS,
DELAWARE, OHIO.

FOR PRESIDENT
GROVER CLEVELAND,
OF NEW YORK.

E PLURIBUS UNUM.

FOR VICE PRESIDENT
ALLEN G. THURMAN,
OF OHIO.

ABOVE: According to the upper left-hand corner of this poster, it's an ad for cigars.

BELOW: A salesman's card displaying two types of Harrison stick pins.

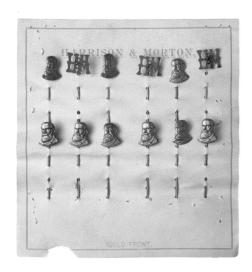

For the fourth time in a row, the election's outcome was in dispute until the end. Cleveland won the popular vote by one hundred thousand ballots but lost the electoral vote, 233 to 168. Again, New York's thirty-six electoral votes, the most of any state, made the difference, and although Cleveland had been governor there, his enemies in Tammany Hall torpedoed his chances.

With Ben Butler on the sidelines and Belva Ann Lockwood's second Equal Rights Party presidential bid a symbolic gesture at best, 1888 marked a significant dip for creative splinter-party objects. The Lockwood candidacy simply updated an old version of her earlier rebus ribbon. More prolific were the Prohibitionists, with nominee Clinton Bowen Fisk featured on several ribbons, tokens, lapel pins, and studs, and a "Dare to Do Right" stickpin.

1892: **Tariff Trouble**

Benjamin Harrison and Grover Cleveland restrung their gloves for a rematch. An early dump-Harrison movement failed to build sufficient support for James G. Blaine, and Harrison's backers won him renomination on the first ballot. Other competition sprang from the Populist Party and their candidate, James B. Weaver.

The Baby Ruth candy bar was named after Cleveland's daughter.

Again, the election turned on the tariff issue, but this time the resounding thud of the botched McKinley Tariff killed the Republicans' chances. Cleveland called attention to its abysmal effect on consumer prices and smugly reminded everyone that he had favored a low tariff for years.

When the votes were tallied, Cleveland won the popular vote by almost four hundred thousand, the largest margin since Grant's election

Candidates in this era threw wild whiskey parties to sway votes. Little commemorative whiskey jugs helped jar partygoers' memories as to which candidate had rendered them drunk the previous evening.

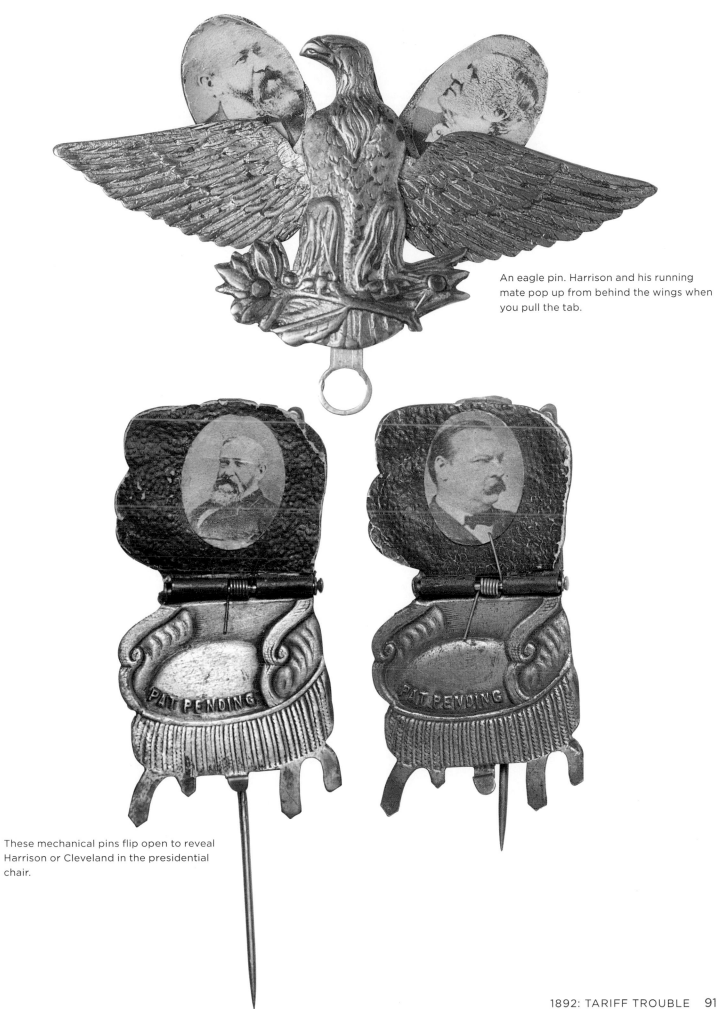

An eagle pin. Harrison and his running mate pop up from behind the wings when you pull the tab.

These mechanical pins flip open to reveal Harrison or Cleveland in the presidential chair.

This darning egg used the election to publicize a clothing company.

President Cleveland's campaign rewarded large donors with these classy ceramic chamber pots.

Grover Cleveland.

Is ready for the 4th of March 1893,

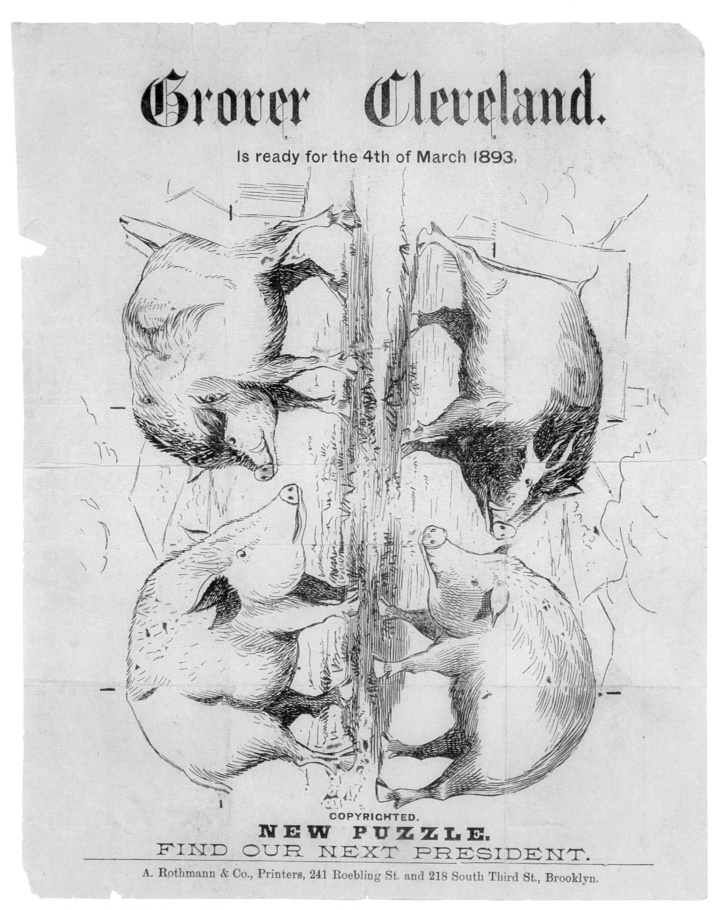

COPYRIGHTED.
NEW PUZZLE.
FIND OUR NEXT PRESIDENT.

A. Rothmann & Co., Printers, 241 Roebling St. and 218 South Third St., Brooklyn.

When this puzzle is folded correctly it
reveals a portrait of Cleveland.

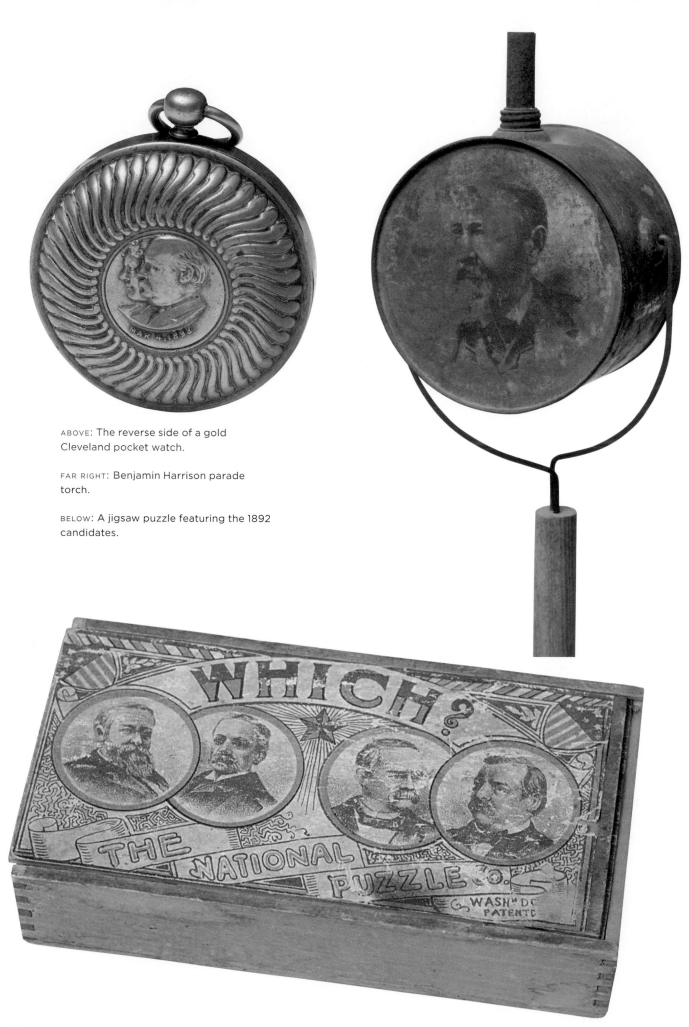

ABOVE: The reverse side of a gold Cleveland pocket watch.

FAR RIGHT: Benjamin Harrison parade torch.

BELOW: A jigsaw puzzle featuring the 1892 candidates.

in 1872. Even so, Weaver faired remarkably well, becoming the first third-party candidate since 1860 to win a state, carrying Colorado, Idaho, Kansas, and Nevada.

The 1892 Harrison-Cleveland rematch spit and sputtered after the excitement of 1888. Harrison attended his dying wife, Cleveland fished in Buzzard's Bay, and voters slept soundly. As a result, the array of campaign objects diminished considerably from previous years. In fact, running the same two candidates led to a blatant recycling of 1888 materials and themes. The only interesting item was the catchy "Tippecanoe and Morton too" banner. (Tippecanoe in reference to a battle won by Harrison's grandfather and Morton in reference to his vice president.)

This Harrison banner references the famous slogan from his grandfather William Henry Harrison's campaign. The Battle of Tippecanoe took place in Indiana in 1811.

1896-1916

In 1868, a billiard ball manufacturer offered a $10,000 prize to anyone who could create a substitute for ivory. Endlessly toiling away into the night in a musky basement in an attempt to win the contest, American inventors John Wesley Hyatt and his brother Isaiah stumbled upon celluloid, the material that would revolutionize campaign trinketry in the dawning century. Twenty-eight years later, Bostonian Amanda M. Lougee patented the celluloid button as we now know it, slapping a printed paper disk under celluloid and sliding it into a metal collet with a fastening device. The less expensive and more durable device allowed for more vivid colors and complicated designs, booting all other lapel doohickeys. Other items peaking in popularity in the new century included watch fobs and satirical political postcards.

A few nose-thumbing novelties from the previous era remained. Soap dolls in cardboard boxes promoted free silver in 1896, but were dismissed soon after, perhaps because people mistook them for babies in coffins. Instead of novelties, campaigns slapped candidates' names on more everyday practical objects like pens, wooden pencils, cigars, ties, aluminum combs, bookmarks, coin purses, and jackknives (you could think fondly of Roosevelt as you parted your hair, or McKinley could ease your frustration as you cut through thick rope). Credit most of the changes to campaign mastermind Mark Hanna. His highly centralized operations shut the doors of local political clubs, abandoning community uniqueness for a sleeker, more uniform attack. He acquired over $3,000,000 in 1896 from Big Business and employed nearly fourteen hundred people, who flooded the country with pamphlets and posters.

ed since 1789.

This Bryan stickpin boasts "Trusts" and "16 to 1" (relating to Bryan's antitrust, prosilver platform) when you open its mouth.

"You shall not press down upon the brow of labor this crown of thorns; you shall not crucify mankind upon a cross of gold," William Jennings Bryan emphatically proclaimed in his acceptance speech at the Democratic convention. But that was Bryan for you, zealously passionate, and he was especially crazy over coinage (making silver the U.S. standard, rather than gold).

Though infamous for his stinker McKinley Tariff, William McKinley of Ohio brought his keen campaigning skills to the Republican convention, and snagged the nomination on the first ballot. Both campaigns focused on Bryan's hot button, the currency issue, which confused party loyalties. Unwilling to support either Bryan's prosilver policies or McKinley's high tariffs, Cleveland (the King Midas of the coinage debate) and his gold-bug Democrats backed their own candidate, John M. Palmer.

The young, empowered Bryan crisscrossed the country, traveling eighteen thousand miles in three months (propelling himself almost exclusively by the hot air he blew during speeches), and amassing tremendous support in the South and West, while McKinley sat around the house per the advice of his campaign manager and puppet master, Mark Hanna. Raising $3,000,000 from

A Bryan prosilver silver bug.

This metal Bryan portrait promotes U.S. expansion.

ABOVE: This sock purse (sixteen times the size of a regular purse) shows how much more efficient the gold standard would be (since its value is sixteen times that of silver). Notice the "Swan Bros." manufacturers are larger than the campaign slogan.

LEFT: This homemade paper product features a portrait of McKinley with a little girl on a chamber pot. I'm not sure what it means, but inclusion of the chamber pot can't bode well for McKinley.

A glance up the posterior of this metal Stanhope pig reveals a portrait of a candidate. An expression at the time was, "In a pig's ass I would vote for McKinley!" or whoever your least favorite candidate might have been.

How did the townspeople know when McKinley would come outside to speak? Jonnie, a friend of McKinley, would blow this horn to announce the upcoming oration.

A McKinley parasol.

RIGHT: This mechanical stickpin showed who was really in charge of McKinley's campaign: Ohio industrialist Mark Hanna. Hanna bobs up and down atop the bike while relegating McKinley and running mate Hobart to the tires.

OPPOSITE: McKinley wanted to place increased taxes on imports to make American manufacturers more competitive in the market.

leading eastern industrialists, Hanna flooded the country with Republican pamphlets written in German, Italian, and Chinese, among other languages, making McKinley the undisputed immigrant choice. By comparison, Bryan raised only $500,000, mostly from the owners of silver mines.

Despite Bryan's prevailing in-person appeal, his target audience of farmers made up less than half of the U.S. population. Buoyed by the growing power of urban manufacturing, McKinley won a decisive victory.

Bryan breathed silver. Ate silver. Slept on a bed of silver, and when he needed to dream about silver for just a few minutes more, hit the silver snooze button

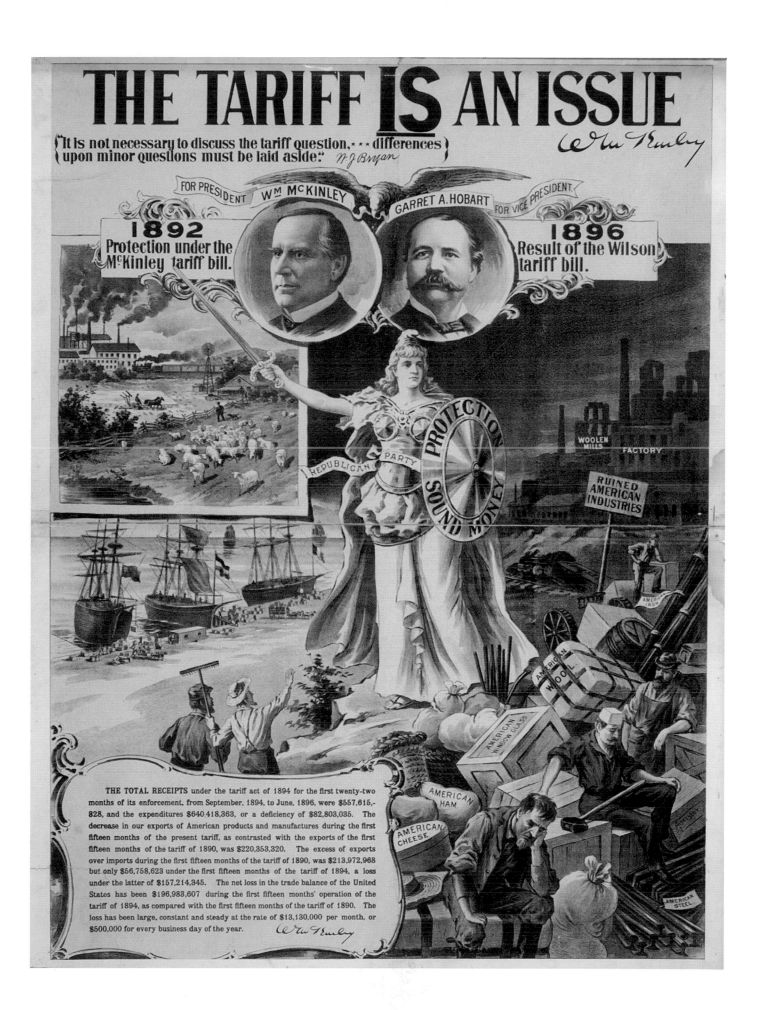

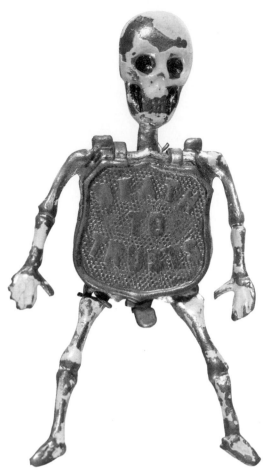

ABOVE: This mechanical skeleton stickpin shows the Democrats' distaste for trusts. The chest opens up to reveal a portrait of McKinley.

ABOVE, RIGHT: Pro-gold standard gold bugs.

on his silver alarm clock. Not since John Fremont's free-soil campaign of 1856 had a candidate focused so stridently upon a single issue. And by zigzagging the nation and showering it in oratory wonder, Bryan left farmers with visions of silverdrops dancing in their heads and inspired a voter turnout exceeding 95 percent in five fiercely contested midwestern states. McKinley was a sluf-off, but Mark Hanna wheeled and dealed behind the scenes, spending monstrous amounts in the defense of the Republican platform of industrial capitalism.

A quick explanation of Bryan's free-silver platform: In 1873, the country had abandoned the bimetallic (gold and silver) monetary system established in 1837, and Bryan wanted it back. According to him, the minting of silver coinage at a value of one sixteenth that of gold would increase the country's money supply and boost the economy. His campaign buttons included "Silver Is Good

Republicans claimed Bryan talked people to death with his epic speeches, spawning these filled coffins.

A McKinley paper lantern.

LEFT: This ensemble was worn during a McKinley torchlight parade.

BELOW: This miniature wooden dinner pail was probably used as an ink well. The 1896 and 1900 Republican "Full Dinner Pail" slogan promoted more jobs and prosperous industry.

Enough for Me," "Silver Should Rule the World," "I Am a Silver Man," even "I Will Carry Silver if It Breaks My Back." And Democrats had no intention of compromising, depicting gold bugs (representing those who preferred gold over silver) being violently impaled by pitchforks, spikes, and silver arrows on many items. McKinley campaign items countered the Bryan silver obsession with gold bugs and gold nugget stickpins baring the legend "Gold Basis." In actuality, McKinley didn't care much about the gold/silver standard argument, preferring the tariff issue.

ABOVE: Celluloid buttons with push-up candidate names.

RIGHT: A shirt front worn during a torchlight parade.

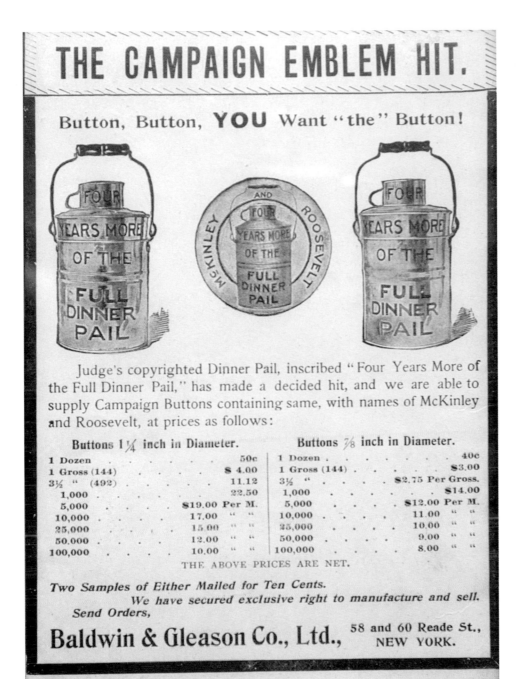

LEFT: An ad for buttons to resell to friends and neighbors.

ABOVE: For the Republicans: "Free silver killed this man."

This unprecedented zealotry made Bryan a sitting duck for Republican sarcasm, some buttons taunting "In McKinley We Trust, In Bryan We Bust." Republicans also reamed the longwinded orator with the legend "Talked to Death" inscribed on buttons and lapel pins tenderly garnished with skeletons, cadavers, and coffins.

By 1900, the Klondike Gold Rush had whisked away the down-and-out depression of the mid-1890s, and the country basked in its newfound prosperity. The citizens associated the good times with President McKinley (even though he had little to do with them), and the Republicans gladly nominated him for a second term.

McKinley needed a new vice president to replace the deceased vice president Garret Hobart. Averse to making decisions, McKinley said he would be more than happy with whomever the convention chose. The Republican delegates picked Spanish-American War hero Theodore Roosevelt, who would soon become the largest political personality of the new century.

McKinley's opponent was once again silver zealot William Jennings Bryan, mostly because the Democrats lacked anyone else with a national reputation. Again, Bryan vehemently insisted that the Democrats include free silver in their platform, and once again he drove away gold Democrats, whose support could have won him the election.

After he returned victorious from the Spanish-American War in the Philippines, a draft Admiral Dewey for President movement emerged. During the

McKinley and Bryan parasols. Bryan's running mate, Adlai Stevenson, was the grandfather of the 1950s presidential candidate. He was also vice president with Grover Cleveland.

A Dewey clock. Vendors sold unassembled clock kits to small businesses, which would assemble and resell them. McKinley and Bryan mates exist.

VOTE FOR
MCKINLEY
AND YOU WILL
WEAR DIAMONDS

REVOLVING BUTTON,

A Catchy Novelty.

OPPOSITE: These inexplicable, creepy-looking soap babies attempted to sway "dad's" vote toward McKinley or Bryan.

campaign that followed, Bryan denounced McKinley for turning the United States into an imperial power by keeping the Philippine Islands after the Spanish-American War. The Republicans said that it was America's duty to bring "civilization" to the nonwhite people who lived there. Meanwhile, lazy McKinley sat around the White House, leaving the energetic whippersnapper Roosevelt to gallivant around the country campaigning. The Republican slogan, "Four More Years of the Full Dinner Pail," emphasized the country's prosperity and carried the party to victory.

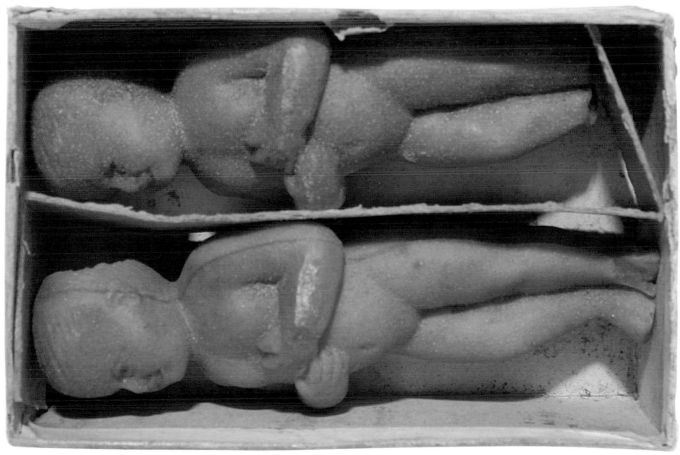

A PROTECTOR OF AMERICAN INDUSTRIES.

An American ⎯⎯⎯⎯⎯
⎯⎯⎯⎯⎯ Paper Napkin,
MANUFACTURED BY
JAPANESE TISSUE MILLS,
SOUTH HADLEY, MASS.

This paper napkin proclaims McKinley
as a "Protector of American Industries."
Notice it was manufactured by Japanese
Tissue Mills.

Placing a lit candle inside this lantern would illuminate the "Dinner Pail" slogan.

The anticlimactic rematch between McKinley and Bryan in 1900 inspired only about half the items of 1896, but at least the political memorabilia of 1900 was more exciting than the election that stimulated it. Celluloids grew even more en vogue, and many of the unusual objects returned: umbrellas, aluminum combs, glass tumblers, pencils, and figural pipes, along with the first few political postcards, watch fobs, tin serving trays, and aluminum pin trays.

Many holier-than-thou Bryan items denounced the Republicans' twin evils of imperialism and trusts. A host of buttons and other items protested McKinley's recent colonial attempts in the Philippines with such mottos as "For the Republic/No Dreams of Empire for the Free." Other items bashed the trusts, vilified McKinley field marshal "Dollar Mark" Hanna, and accused McKinley of selling out to Big Business.

McKinley's new items capitalized on the booming economy and the patriotic response to a "splendid little war" (the Spanish-American War), portraying him

as the architect of the economic revival and Roosevelt as a war hero. Teddy's Rough Rider image revolted the refined Mark Hanna, but he commissioned buttons with Roosevelt in uniform and hat just the same.

However, the bread and butter of the campaign was the full dinner pail, emphasizing prosperity and targeting blue-collar voters. (Why was everyone eating out of pails?) Ribbons and at least a dozen styles of buttons featured pail designs, the most imaginative of them reading, "Do You Smoke? Yes—Since 1896! That's What McKinley Promised" and depicting a smoking factory in the shape of a dinner pail. Metal-pail parade lanterns appeared, one with cut-outs to read "Four Years More of the Full Dinner Pail" when the device was lit.

With a total solar eclipse appearing on May 28, 1900, commercial political minds found a way to exploit the astronomical sight for campaign fodder. A variety of buttons depicted Bryan eclipsing McKinley or McKinley eclipsing Bryan, accompanied by such predictions as "Total Eclipse Nov. 6" or "Partial Eclipse/ Will Be Total in November."

McKinley ran unopposed within his own party and Bryan received a second Democratic nomination almost by default, so there was little hope for splinter parties. However, Prohibition Party candidate John Granville Woolley's campaign pieces damned both major parties, insisting, "A vote for the Republican Party is a vote for 'booze' in the dinner pail" and "A vote for the Democratic Party is a vote for a dinner pail full of 'booze.'"

This button unkindly compares William J. Bryan to Emilio Aguinaldo, rebel leader of the Philippines force during the Spanish-American War, and Boss Croaker of Tammany Hall.

Following McKinley's assassination, the public took to their new presidential Teddy like a four-year-old to a new toy. But to earn the 1904 nomination, Roosevelt had to charm a tough crowd of stick-in-the-muds known as the Republican Party. They saw Teddy as an unruly adolescent, and would have preferred the clean-cut smartie Mark Hanna. When Hanna died of typhoid fever in February, however, the Republicans begrudgingly nominated Roosevelt.

> **Roosevelt was the first president to fly in an airplane.**

Traditionally, the Republican Party favored Big Business, while the Democrats supported more reform-minded progressive candidates. Because Roosevelt was himself a Progressive, the Democrats were at a loss. In the end, they decided to nominate a conservative candidate, Judge Alton Parker of New York, in hopes of catering to disenfranchised Republican voters.

The political confusion led to one of the greatest landslides in American presidential history. The cocky Roosevelt had expected to win, but not by such an overwhelming margin. "My dear," he told his second wife, Edith, flashing one of his famous toothy grins, "I am no longer a political accident."

The lopsided victory of Theodore Roosevelt over a virtually catatonic Alton B. Parker (who spent the whole campaign in seclusion at his home in Ulster County, New York, setting an example apparently followed by most of his

RIGHT: A Parker and Davis metal scale.

OPPOSITE: A cutout mask of Roosevelt.

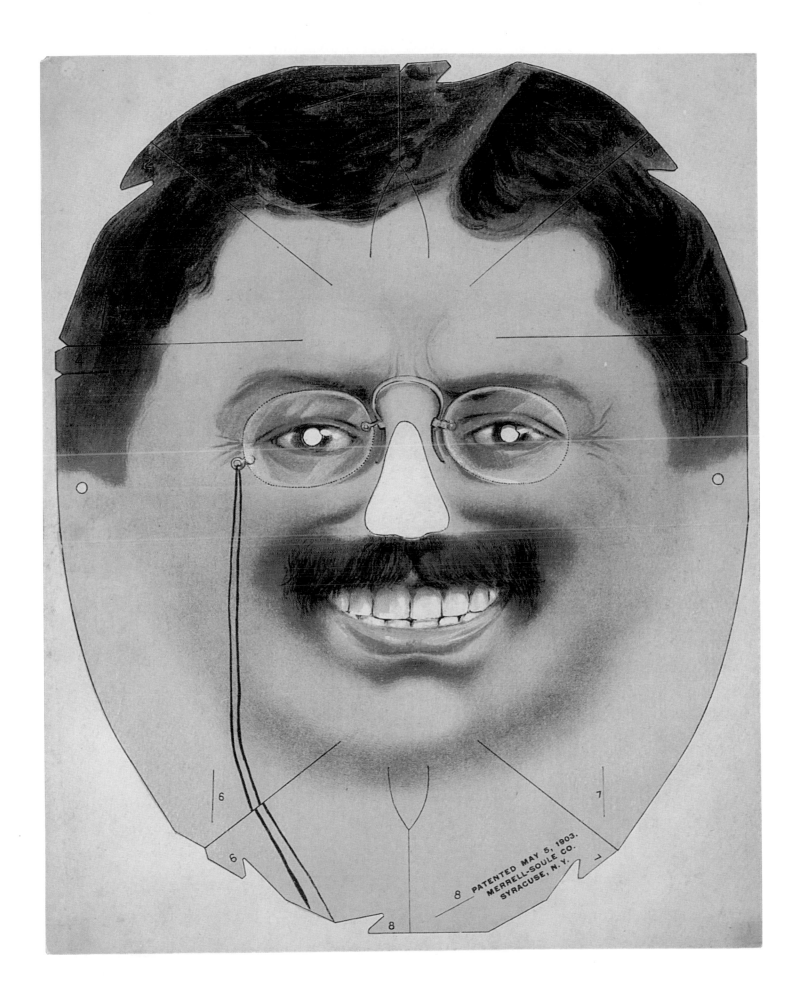

Fabric lapel flowers imprinted with the McKinley-Hobart ticket and Roosevelt.

ABOVE: A Parker clip-on tie.

Teddy's Rough Riders.

supporters) and several splinter-party candidates inspired a plentiful array of the usual buttons and posters, along with my two favorites: canes (if you can't make it to the polling place on your own two feet, the candidate you support will support you) and scissors.

Repeating the strategy of 1900, many 1904 Roosevelt items referenced his fame as the war hero who led his Rough Riders up San Juan Hill, featuring the big guy in uniform, astride his galloping charger, complete with windblown hair for a heroically sexy look. Politically themed objects paid homage to Roosevelt's triumphant Square Deal, gracing coin purses with the slogan "Give Every Man a Square Deal." (Why Republicans wanted to Give Every Man a Coin Purse is beyond my comprehension.)

In 1901, Roosevelt had invited black educator Booker T. Washington to the White House for dinner. Two years later, Charles H. Thomas, a white Chicago Republican, had grand delusions of impressing upon "the colored brothers that the only way to the higher life was to vote the Republican ticket." Thomas commissioned a lithographed print with a matching button depicting the two men at table, with "Equality" inscribed boldly on the tablecloth. Sounds harmless, right? Soon, thousands of black men in Chicago were sporting the buttons, spawning a riotous white-supremacist backlash. Of course, party leaders tried to appease everybody. They disavowed the buttons to please the racists, and made a weak attempt to not alienate black supporters by ordering another "Equality" button, this one depicting Roosevelt leading black soldiers up San Juan Hill.

The yawn-worthy Democratic items featured only the names and likenesses of their two old unsightly and unimpressive nominees, Parker and his octogenarian running mate, Henry Gassaway Davis, due to

ABOVE: A print of Roosevelt with his Rough Riders during the Mexican-American War.

BELOW: A flexible Roosevelt ceramic toy doll.

A mechanical tin portrait of Roosevelt. When you open his mouth, it reads "Give them hell, boys!"

Roosevelt aboard a mechanical horse
which bucks him back and forth.

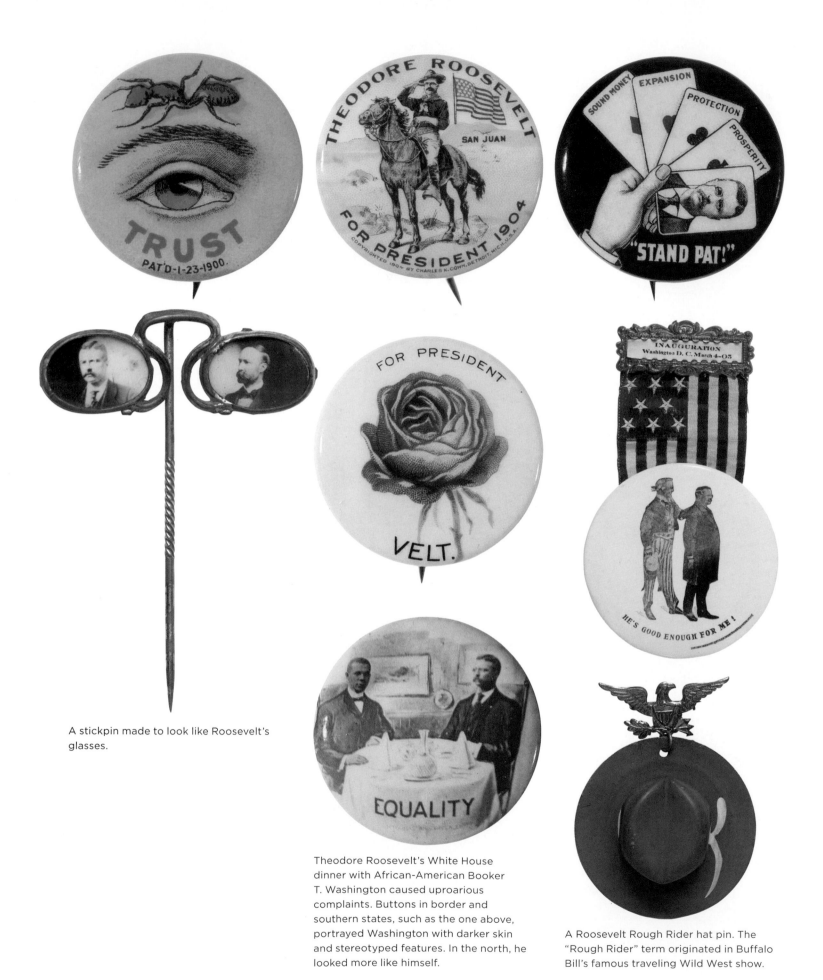

A stickpin made to look like Roosevelt's glasses.

Theodore Roosevelt's White House dinner with African-American Booker T. Washington caused uproarious complaints. Buttons in border and southern states, such as the one above, portrayed Washington with darker skin and stereotyped features. In the north, he looked more like himself.

A Roosevelt Rough Rider hat pin. The "Rough Rider" term originated in Buffalo Bill's famous traveling Wild West show.

the failure of the campaign to establish any thematic focus. (At age eighty, Davis was [and remains] the oldest person nominated on a major party ticket.)

Nineteen hundred four proved to be a weak year for third-party memorabilia as well. Socialist candidate Eugene Debs invited the "Workers of the World [to] Unite," while Harrisburg, Pennsylvania Prohibitionist Silas Comfort Swallow used bird wordplays on his name, and urged his supporters to "Use Maple City Soap." (My contribution would have been "Swallow Your Pride. You Have No Chance of Actually Winning.")

This Roosevelt and Fairbanks parasol was awarded to large contributors.

All kinds of stars owe their "I'm going to retire at the top of my game, change my mind, then come back and be half as good as I once was" shtick to the original renege-er, Theodore Roosevelt. During the 1904 campaign, Teddy had announced that "under no circumstances" would he run for president again, but when 1908 rolled around, he badly wanted to stay. At forty-nine, he was the same chipper, rebellious lad who had bulldozed through last election's fuddy-duddy challengers. But bound to his word, he prepared to leave office.

Roosevelt chose his secretary of war, William Howard Taft, as his successor, ensuring Taft the Republican nomination. In the Democratic camp, the embarrassing loss suffered by Alton Parker returned power to the party's populist wing, and William Jennings Bryan won nomination for the third time in four elections.

Taft was the only president to also serve as Chief Justice of the Supreme Court.

Detailed tin tray with past Republican presidential nominees bordering Taft and Sherman.

WILLIAM H. TAFT

OUR NEXT PRESIDENT

To give the brilliant speaker some credit, the issues he championed (women's suffrage and income tax) would eventually become law, but the country was not ready for the would-be prophet's crusade for change. Taft promised to finish what Teddy had started, and rode his mentor's popularity to victory.

The 1908 Bryan-Taft bout saw some beautiful items (a number of multicolor buttons imitating the Art Nouveau style of artist Maxfield Parrish) and some unusual innovations such as tip trays (commonly used in saloons) reminded drunkards to vote for Taft and Sherman and to pay their exorbitant tabs.

A few 1908 Bryan items attempted to bring out his poor Nebraskan upbringing with the inscription "The Nation's Commoner," although Bryan was

A Taft pennant.

An impartial fan passed out at bars to promote voting and discourage brawling.

Taft was often caricaturized as a billy goat, correlating in some regard to his first name, Bill.

LEFT: This Billibois toy made you one of Billy (Taft's) Boys. My favorite line from the poem on the box reads, ". . . my weight is mighty,/I'll get votes by the pound."

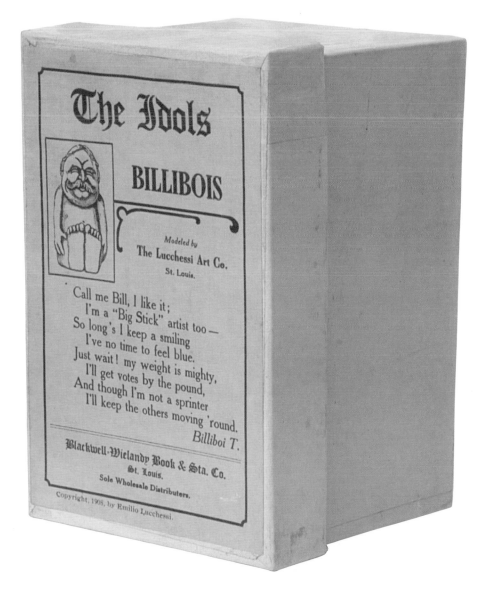

A Taft-Sherman belt buckle.

Copyrighted 1908—I. N. Co.-Chicago

WHO IS GOING TO WIN THE RACE?

WHITE HOUSE

Roll wheels on table and see candidates run

A postcard with candidates "running" for office.

far from the bread line. They also inflated his already bloated ego with a button throwing his mug alongside the faces of Washington, Jefferson, Jackson, and Lincoln, boasting all to be "Enemies of Special Privilege/Upholders of Equality Before the Law."

The Democrats followed the subsequent trail of logic in developing their anti-Taft items: Taft is fat. Fat jokes are funny. Therefore, Taft fat jokes are funny. Items poking fun at Taft's monumental girth included the harsh "Nobody Loves a Fat Man" caricature buttons, and postcards insisting "No Extra Large Chairs Needed at the White House" and "330 Pounds—Not Electoral Votes."

Although an "A Big Man for a Big Party" linen handkerchief tried to turn Taft's rotundity into a virtue, he was not a jolly fat man, and his characterless persona drew the focus of most Taft items toward either his opponent or his popular predecessor. Republicans did much to promote Bryan's glowing reputation as a perpetual loser crackpot windbag. Items exploiting Taft's position as Theodore Roosevelt's chosen heir included the acrostic "T-ake A-dvice F-rom T-eddy." Also, Taft's nickname "Billy Possum" (although Billy Whale would have been more appropriate), gave rise to possum clothing buttons, fobs, and postcards. One could even aspire to become a member of the "Possum Club."

A metal elephant (Republican mascot) with a celluloid Taft on its back.

If you want a country run right, you should just run it yourself. Theodore Roosevelt's opinion of President William Howard Taft had deteriorated exponentially by 1912 and he saw no logical choice but to dethrone his protégé. Roosevelt and Taft engaged in a vicious struggle for the top spot at the Republican convention, and although Roosevelt was a darling among voters, Taft wielded more influence with the party leaders, giving him the Republican nod.

Roosevelt didn't know how to do anything quietly, let alone lose graciously. If the Republicans wouldn't endorse him, he would just have to endorse himself. Perpetually looking through "Roose"-tinted glasses, Teddy formed his own political party, the Progressives, specifically to nominate himself for the presidency. Roosevelt's claim that he was as "strong as a bull moose," led many to refer to Teddy's new baby as the Bull Moose Party.

The third candidate, somewhat lost in the Republican catfight, was Democratic nominee Woodrow Wilson, who was not an imposing figure or exciting personality, but stood to gain exponentially from the chaos in the Republican camp. In a race as tight as a 30-inch waist on Taft, Wilson triumphed thanks to his portly challenger,

> Wilson was the first president to hold a press conference.

ABOVE: A metal pin from the Bull Moose Progressive ticket of Roosevelt and Johnson.

RIGHT: This metal mechanical bank references Roosevelt's hunting trip to Africa when he killed over 1,200 animals, most of which are now in taxidermy form at the the Museum of Natural History in New York. When Roosevelt shoots a coin into the tree, a bear pops out. Oddly, there are no bears in Africa.

Roosevelt and Johnson

"*For there is neither East nor West,*
Border nor Breed nor Birth,
When two strong men stand face to face
Though they come from the ends of the earth."
—Kipling

When you blew into this metal whistle, it looked as if you were sporting Roosevelt's trademark pearly whites.

who took away just enough votes from the Bull Moose. Taft finished a distant, humiliating third.

Theodore Roosevelt's bull-headed Bull Moose campaign, along with the major party bids of Taft and Democrat Woodrow Wilson and a surprisingly respectable showing by Socialist Eugene Debs, produced the first truly exciting presidential race since 1896. Yet somehow, the campaign items failed to reflect the enthusiasm.

Taft, in the midst of a sour-tasting presidency, with such 1908 leftovers as "Billy Possum" and "Smilin' Bill," and with zero chance of aligning himself with his now-rival Roosevelt, had dug himself a hole, and fat men do not get out of holes easily. His campaign items could do nothing but invoke party members to stick with him, with buttons reading "Good Republicans Don't Bolt a Party Ticket" and "Unconditional Republican Club."

With the Republicans divided, all Democrat Wilson had to do was not rock the boat. Wilson trinkets skirted issues in favor of "Wood-Row" rowboat wordplays and such commonplace slogans as "Win with Wilson," "Man of the Hour," and "Pride of New Jersey," which probably didn't do much for the rest of the country.

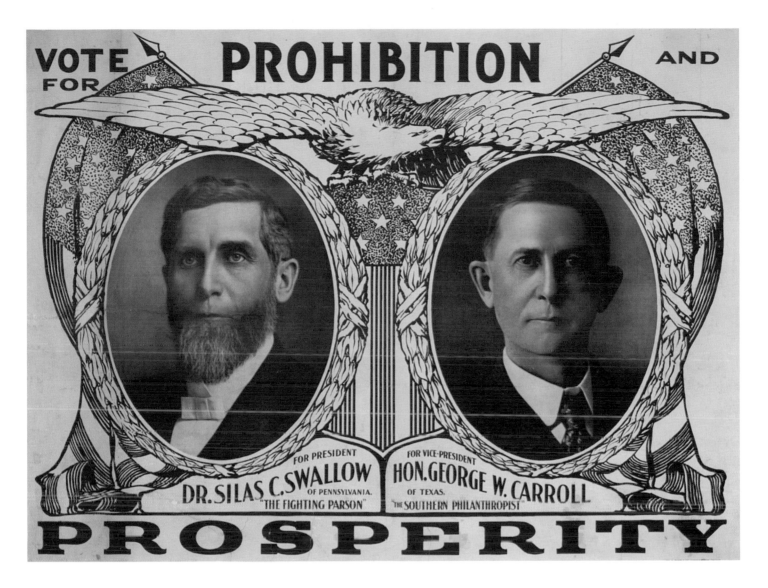

VOTE FOR **PROHIBITION** AND

FOR PRESIDENT
DR. SILAS C. SWALLOW OF PENNSYLVANIA.
"THE FIGHTING PARSON"

FOR VICE-PRESIDENT
HON. GEORGE W. CARROLL OF TEXAS.
"THE SOUTHERN PHILANTHROPIST"

PROSPERITY

Roosevelt owed the strongest third-party campaign in history to his marketable celebrity persona, echoed in teddy bears eerily decked in his famous teeth and glasses (a scary sight, indeed) and items adorned with his "Bull Moose" and "Dee-lighted" catchphrases. Some inscriptions reminded voters of his return, such as "My Hat is in the Ring" (during the primaries and Republican convention) or "My Hat Is STILL in the Ring" (during the general election), but ended up reading as painful reminders that Roosevelt had overstayed his welcome.

The Prohibition candidates for president and vice president in 1912. Their platform precluded drinking, dancing, and men and women living together except to procreate—even when married.

The first tab—cheap metal die-cut worn on your lapel—created for presidential campaigns. Now it is possible to mass produce ten million at a time.

At their 1916 convention, the peace loving Democrats renominated Woodrow Wilson and unveiled their slogan, "He Kept Us Out of War," intending to ride their opposition to entry into World War I back to the White House. The Republicans challenged their gutless competitors with Supreme Court Justice Charles Evans Hughes, who had all intentions of lighting a fire under the U.S. military and crusading into Europe, but only if the situation warranted action, of course. The candidates both wanted to ban child labor and give support to women's suffrage, so the race boiled down to either "give the Germans hell" or "wish the Germans well."

Many newspapers predicted a Hughes victory, but the morning after the balloting, California's electoral votes remained in the air. Finally, California went Democratic, reelecting the antiwar Wilson.

Nineteen sixteen produced the poorest selection of presidential memorabilia of any presidential campaign since 1880, an indication that perhaps the material culture of the late nineteenth century was a dying phenomenon. Hughes's memorabilia abandoned direct reference to the war in favor of the patriotically vague "Undiluted Americanism" and "For Law and Liberty." The items shied from issues in order to please both old guard conservatives and Bull Moose progressives, crooning "Republicans/Bull Moosers/Get Together" (which would have been a great slow-dance tune title at a party mixer), and displaying the

A Wilson tobacco tin.

YOUR PRESIDENT.

"I am willing, no matter what my personal fortunes may be, to play for the verdict of mankind."—Woodrow Wilson.

PEACE AND PROSPERITY
ARE YOURS!
WOODROW WILSON'S
GREAT RECORD:

Federal Reserve Bank Law
Farm Loan Law
8-Hour Day Law

Workmen's Compensation Law
Child Labor Law
Anti-Injunction Law
An Inheritance Tax Law
Railway Safety Law
Parcels Post Improved
Postoffice Self-Supporting
Seamen's Welfare Law

Tariff Revised Downward
Agricultural Extension Law
Nonpartisan Tariff Commission Law
Income Tax Law
Good Roads Law
Merchant Marine Law
Grain Gambling Stopped
Anti-Trust Law Strengthened
War Risk Insurance Law
Children's Bureau

Law Preventing Dumping of European made goods into this country at the close of the war.

Law Giving President Power to Retaliate Against Foreign Governments which Violate American Rights.

OUR FIRST REAL "PREPAREDNESS"
TO INSURE CONTINUANCE OF PEACE

"UPON THIS RECORD WE GO TO THE COUNTRY"

HOME SHOW PRINTING HOUSE — KANSAS CITY, MO.

A metal stool with an engraved portrait of Hughes and Fairbanks on the seat.

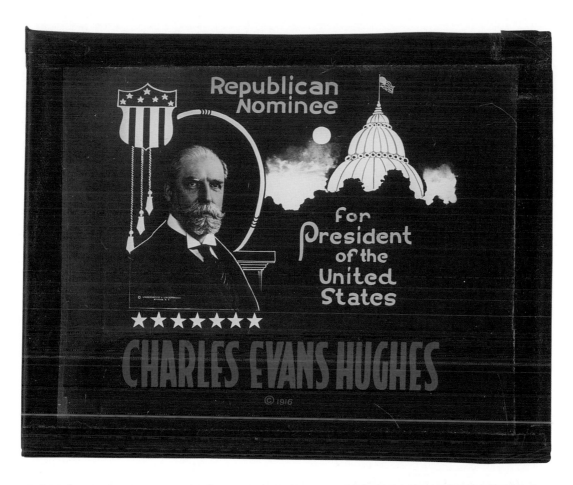

Colored glass slides featuring
photographs of the Republican nominees.

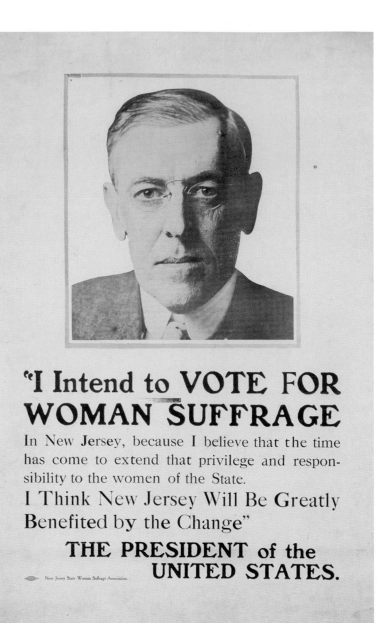

"I Intend to VOTE FOR WOMAN SUFFRAGE

In New Jersey, because I believe that the time has come to extend that privilege and responsibility to the women of the State.

I Think New Jersey Will Be Greatly Benefited by the Change"

THE PRESIDENT of the UNITED STATES.

New Jersey State Woman Suffrage Association.

The publishers of these two newspapers reported the election results before late vote totals from California would hand the presidency to Wilson.

Republican elephant and Progressive bull moose living side by side in blissful harmony on campaign buttons.

Wilson's objects did everything to exploit his peaceful stance (other than releasing masses of doves toting olive branches), with buttons proclaiming "War in Europe/Peace in America/ God Bless Wilson" and the wimpy "Safety First." Wilson items also introduced the catchy and ambivalent slogan "America First" (as if America barely made it into the Republican top five) on many buttons, some reading "They Have Kept the Faith/We'll Stand by Them/America First," and "America First/Thank God for Wilson," which sounds positive without really saying anything at all.

A Wilson ceramic tile. Perfect for any bathroom or kitchen.

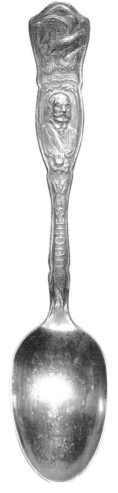

A Hughes spoon.

Voter turnout, along with political party membership, took a deafening nosedive in the years after World War I. The public was distracted by radio, motion pictures, and the automobile. Although new media brought the faces and voices of candidates to an ever-expanding audience, the only American political figure to challenge the celebrity status of Babe Ruth and Rudolph Valentino was Franklin Delano Roosevelt, with some help from his radio "fireside chats."

Despite this decline in campaign interest, most trinkets maintained their volume, just becoming cheaper and tackier—meant to be given away, not sold. Though all the rage in 1896, the celluloid button had a new challenger: lithographed tin. These "lithos" could not provide the aesthetic detail of their predecessor, but made up for it in cost-effectiveness. Paper items on the whole dropped, but posters prospered, illuminating telephone poles with bright political exuberance. Grassroots activities fizzled, save for the new door-to-door method, with supporters hanging John W. Davis teapot logos and Alf Landon sunflower signs on neighborhood doorknobs. The large political bill-

KEEP COOLIDGE

UB OF PLYMOUTH, VERMONT

Keep Coolidge

Music by
BRUCE HARPER

BY W. B. Tuttle,
All rights, including that of public performance

SECOND VICE PRESIDENT
GEORGE W. FRINK
PLYMOUTH, VT.

SECRETARY
DICK P. BROWN
PLYMOUTH, VT.

MRS. LAURA JOHNSON
PLYMOUTH, VT.

IDA CHEEVER GOODWIN
BRUCE HARPER

or Coolidge

board made its grand entrance around 1940, the original depicting
an innocent little girl asking, "Daddy, what's a Democracy?" and
receiving the cringe-inducing explanation, "It's America with Willkie!"
Nineteen twenty welcomed women into the political fold for the
first time, and Republicans pounced on the chance to court them,
introducing compact celluloid mirrors requesting "the lady on
the other side" to cast votes for Warren Harding, Calvin Coolidge,
and Herbert Hoover. Sadly, domestic items including thimbles and
needle packs, featuring such slogans as "Hoover-Home-Happiness,"
remind us that equality was far from complete.

The automobile provided a brand-new outlet for campaigners'
creativity, including spare tire covers (before designers moved the tire
to the trunk) featuring huge images of candidates' faces, making them
the clear precursor to bus and cab ads. Bumper stickers didn't
come around until the 1950s, but license attachments wrapped
party platforms around your existing license plate and
nonadhesive banners boasted "A Carload of Willkie Votes."

One of the rarest buttons in my collection. Because the Democrats didn't stand a chance against the powerhouse Republican ticket, buttons for them were never mass-produced. This button is only a sample.

Harding was the first president to speak over the radio.

With Woodrow Wilson's health on the rocks, the Democrats tried to copy the popular two-term president with clone-like accuracy. They nominated Ohio Governor James M. Cox, who was eager to ride the Wilson bandwagon, and his running mate Franklin D. Roosevelt, chosen because of his famous last name and affiliation with Wilson's cabinet.

The nomination from the Republicans came not from a convention, but from Suite 404 of the Blackstone Hotel in Chicago. In a meeting recalling images from a two-tone *noir* flick, deadlocked party bosses convened secretly, smoke-filled-room-style, to work out a deal. At two in the morning, the men called in potential nominee Warren G. Harding, and (as the seedy jazz sax built to a crescendo) inquired if he had anything to hide. Harding thought for ten minutes and replied, "No." The next day, he was nominated. (Now if it takes a guy ten minutes to ponder his answer to that question, wouldn't that give you pause?)

As Cox campaigned on the peaceful and progressive reforms of Wilson's record, the Republicans railed against it. They claimed Wilson had been unprepared for World War I, and lambasted his cherished League of Nations. Following a devastating war, the voting public was in no mood for Cox's idealism, and rallied behind Harding's campaign slogan, which offered a "Return to Normalcy." The

Cox-Roosevelt watch fob.

A delegate from Indiana wore this at the Republican Convention.

HARDING
FOR PRESIDENT 1920

A homemade Harding pin with a bell.

FOR PRESIDENT
JAMES M. COX

A Harding beanie.

1856-1920

Fremont
Lincoln
Harding
Veteran Club

Lancaster County
Pa.

UNDER
The 19th
Amendment
I CAST MY
FIRST VOTE
Nov. 2nd, 1920

Harding
Coolidge

The Straight
Republican
Ticket

Lancaster, Pa.

This purse was one of many items targeting women voters in the first election since women's suffrage.

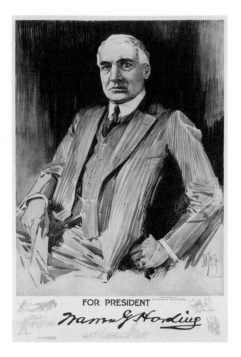

FOR PRESIDENT

Warren G. Harding

FOR PRESIDENT

Warren G. Harding

FOR VICE PRESIDENT

Calvin Coolidge

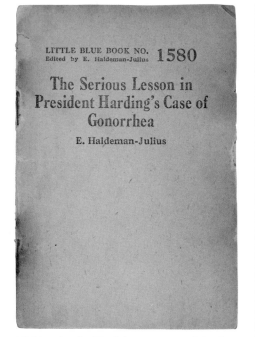

LITTLE BLUE BOOK NO. 1580
Edited by E. Haldeman-Julius

The Serious Lesson in
President Harding's Case of
Gonorrhea

E. Haldeman-Julius

Written (and edited) by unaccomplished hack writer E. Haldeman Julius and published by Harding's spiteful father-in-law, this book sought to destroy Harding's reputation. The only evidence behind the claim is circumstantial. Harding died under suspicious circumstances on a trip along the West Coast. Of the disease? We'll never know for sure.

RIGHT: This proclamation from a Maine polling place attempted to dissuade citizens from selling their votes.

STATE OF MAINE

Penalty for Selling Vote

(Revised Statutes, Chap. 7, Sec. 97)

Whoever shall offer, or promise, or agree to receive any money or other valuable consideration for giving in his vote at any election held under the provisions of the Constitution or of this chapter, and shall in accordance with such offer, promise or agreement, give in his vote at such election, shall be fined not more than one hundred dollars, or imprisoned not more than one year, and shall be excluded from the right of suffrage for a term of ten years.

EDGAR C. SMITH, Secretary of State

Republicans, on the wings of the soon-to-be scandal-ridden Harding, won in a landslide.

The 1920 campaign inspired a rather limited material response, but did include a Cox-Roosevelt jigsaw puzzle (I can't think of a better way to spend my Sunday afternoon) as well as the extraordinarily classy Harding mechanical nose-thumber.

The Democrats unintentionally chose to back some odd issues, with one button making the bizarre request to "Americanize America," an inappropriate slogan (whatever its intended meaning) for a party so heavily dependent upon the immigrant vote. Another, "Cox and Cocktails," promoted Cox's anti-Prohibition stance, but awkwardly associated Cox with alcohol.

Although the Republicans bashed Wilson and his League of Nations, they blatantly stole his "America First" slogan of 1916, with Harding cigar packs and window decals reading "Think of America First" and "America Always First/ Back to Normal/Law & Order." But at least the Republicans used the ambiguous catchphrase with a clear message: Stay out of other countries' business.

OUR CANDIDATE

EUGENE V. DEBS
Convict No. 9653

This poster shows Eugene V. Debs, the only presidential candidate in U.S. history who ran for office from prison. How did he land in the slammer? Trying to organize a railroad servers' union, which would be completely legal today.

When the country is at peace and prosperous, as in 1924, reelection for the incumbent president should be easy like Sunday morning. Upright citizen Calvin Coolidge won the nomination, although some Republicans feared voters would associate Coolidge with the scandal-plagued Warren Harding.

The Democrats had a much more difficult time making up their minds, in fact, the most difficult time in history. For more than one hundred ballots, Californian William McAdoo, the rural choice, and New York governor Alfred E. Smith, the urban choice, remained deadlocked. (You would think after the first fifty ballots or so that they would know the tie was coming. "Wow, fellow delegate, a tie on the eighty-seventh ballot, too!") In the end, McAdoo and Smith both withdrew, handing the nomination to West Virginia lawyer John W. Davis on the 103rd ballot.

The Progressive Party candidate, rebel Republican senator Robert M. La Follette launched an impressive third-party assault, snatching 17 percent of the popular vote, but in the end, Coolidge put both La Follette and Davis on ice.

The central campaign question of 1924: Could Coolidge overcome the Harding administration's Teapot Dome scandal? Corruption was not new to the presidency, by any means, but the Teapot Dome was the most public presidential

ABOVE: The first automobile license plate accessories.

OPPOSITE: A weekly newsletter distributed by the president to inform citizens about White House events.

BOY SCOUTS OF AMERICA
WEEKLY PICTORIAL OF NATIONAL ACTIVITIES

SCOUTING PAYS ITS RESPECTS AT WHITE HOUSE

President Coolidge, and picked Boy Scouts of Washington, D. C., representing all Scoutdom on recent occasion of the 14th Anniversary of the Scout Movement when these lads called at the White House to pay their respects to the nation's Chief Executive, who is also the Honorary President of the Boy Scout organization.

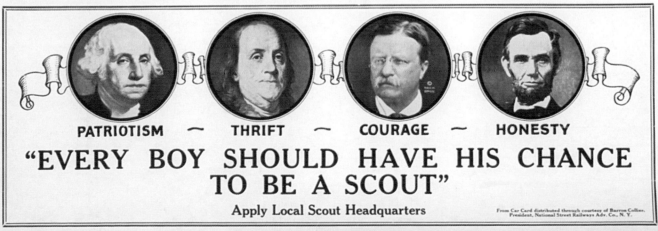

PATRIOTISM ~ THRIFT ~ COURAGE ~ HONESTY

"EVERY BOY SHOULD HAVE HIS CHANCE TO BE A SCOUT"

Apply Local Scout Headquarters

From Car Card distributed through courtesy of Barron Collier, President, National Street Railways Adv. Co., N. Y.

ELLIOTT SERVICE CO., NEW YORK, SOLE PRODUCERS

Music and lyrics to "Keep Cool and Keep Coolidge" campaign theme.

A Coolidge fan to keep you cool.

This race was one of the best for the Communist Party, perhaps because of this poster's strong image: a red muscular worker rather than the normal Communist image of beleaguered huddled masses.

RIGHT: A Davis-Bryan crossword puzzle stamp.

iniquity up to that time. Its name derived from a rock overlooking some federally-owned Wyoming oil fields, which Secretary of the Interior Albert Fall leased to Pan Am Petroleum in exchange for illegal gifts. La Follette capitalized on the major role he had played in the scandal's investigation, with a "C'mon Bob Let's Go!" Progressive button offering the choice of La Follette or a teapot. (Honestly, Bob, it depends on what kind of tea. I love Earl Grey.)

The Democratic promotion of John Davis produced the smallest number of items from a major party since Reconstruction, possibly due to the lethargy surrounding their compromise candidate, but mostly because the Democrats poured their entire campaign efforts into the Teapot. One button featured a GOP elephant simmering in a "Teapot Dome" teapot, while another invited violent voters to "Take a Kick at the Teapot."

Although the Republican "Keep Cool with Coolidge" campaign invoked ideas of cold temperatures (some Coolidge stamps featured electric table fans) and images of a Joe Cool-ish hipster, "Silent Cal" was more bio-lab geek than rebel without a cause. In an era of flappers and bathtub gin, the nerdy ultraconservative Coolidge loved to sleep and abhorred activist leadership, leading to "Careful Cautious Calvin Coolidge" postcards and "Safe-Sane-

LEFT: This stickpin for Davis reminded voters of Harding's scandal and encouraged them to associate it with the Republican Coolidge.

Steady" posters. The Clark Kents of the country rallied around this relatable nerd, wanting to stay "Safe with Cal," as one button put it. (It's a shame the Republicans didn't market Coolidge pocket protectors.) When told of Coolidge's death in 1933, Dorothy Parker replied, "How could you tell?"

A Robert M. La Follette poster. LaFollette, a former Republican governor and senator in Wisconsin, ran for president under the Progressive Party, and carried his home state along with 17 percent of the national popular vote.

When President Calvin Coolidge decided to call it quits after one term, Secretary of Commerce Herbert Hoover became the second consecutive Republican candidate with alliterated first and last names. To challenge the shy, humble Hoover, the Democrats nominated the colorful New York governor Alfred E. Smith.

Smith was the first Roman Catholic to be nominated for president by a major political party, and bigoted Republicans printed pamphlets claiming that if elected, Smith would turn over rule of the country to the Vatican. Smith entertained huge enthusiastic crowds in the East, but bumpkin Protestants in the Midwest and West bought the intolerant Popish hogwash, and denounced Smith. Hoover's modest campaign, coupled with the Smith backlash, led to Hoover carrying forty of the forty-eight states.

The 1928 contest yielded some of the most creative items in years, including the clever enamel "Hoo but Hoover" owls and

> **Hoover was the first president to have a telephone right on his desk.**

RIGHT: Metal stove burner covers for both candidates.

OPPOSITE: Herbert Hoover first gained notoriety for helping to remove the blockade against Germany and organize a moratorium on debt after World War I, saving Germany from imminent financial disaster.

PHILADELPHIA GAZETTE-DEMOKRAT

What Herbert Hoover Did for Germany

Herbert Hoover, immediately after the Armistice and before the Treaty of Versailles was signed, brought about the cancellation of the blockade against Germany in order to make possible the supplying of the suffering people in Germany with food. This was done after bringing down the long resistance of the allied statesmen.

Herbert Hoover was the founder and organizer of the great American move to feed the German children. This great act of charity was kept up during almost two years, and it certainly saved the then coming generation in Germany.

Herbert Hoover, in 1925, stood with all his energy for the

conclusion of a treaty of commerce with Germany.

Herbert Hoover, in 1931, came out for the regulation of political debts, including a moratorium for Germany. He, at this time, without doubt saved the Reich from financial disaster.

Herbert Hoover, by advising Europe to put her financial structure in order, indirectly started the conference of Lausanne, during which Germany was liberated from those unbearable reparations.

Herbert Hoover is the man on whom Germany, who is still wrestling with grave economical and financial problems, will have to depend in the future.

The Republicans of Pennsylvania Are Against Prohibition

The State Committee of the Republican Party came out for the cancellation of the Eighteenth Amendment and for the modification of the Volstead Act. The organization of the Republican Party in Philadelphia declared itself in favor of repeal of the state prohibition enforcement laws (Snyder Act). All the representatives of Philadelphia in the State Senate and in the State House of Representatives are for repeal of prohibition. All the representatives in the State Senate and in the National House of Representatives are "wet."

Leading Republican Candidates in the State

For Auditor General

HON. FRANK E. BALDWIN

Born in McKean County, 1866.

Graduate of public schools, St. Bonaventure's College, and University of Michigan.

Lawyer, Bank President, former School Director, Burgess, and Postmaster at Austin, Pa.

Twenty years a member of Pennsylvania State Senate.

Supported Mothers' Assistance, Workmen's Compensation, Public Roads, Service Men and Public School Improvement programs.

President pro tempore of Senate, 1921.

As Chairman of the Finance Committee of the Senate for seven sessions has acquired thorough working knowledge of State's fiscal problems.

For State Treasurer

HON. CHARLES A. WATERS

Born in Philadelphia, 1892.

Educated at St. Joseph's College and University of Pennsylvania.

Admitted to Philadelphia Bar 1916.

Entered First Officers' Training Camp, at Fort Niagara, May, 1917, and served in the Army during the World War until honorably discharged in January, 1919.

Served as Assistant Chief and later Chief of Bureau of Corporations, Department of the Auditor General, 1922 to 1924 when he was made Special Deputy Auditor General.

Appointed Secretary of Labor and Industry by Governor John S. Fisher.

Elected Auditor General in November, 1928.

Men who throughout their public life have proved themselves worthy of every confidence of the citizenry of Pennsylvania.
Both Senator Baldwin and Auditor General Waters know their native State, its People and their needs. Both have declared against any tax increase, and in favor of reduced costs of State government.

RIGHT: This ad featuring Henry Ford was the first time a celebrity publicly endorsed a candidate.

OPPOSITE: A Smith Democratic convention poster.

Henry Ford
Tells why he's
For Hoover

*The revolution in industry * * * is only beginning. Some people think we are now in the industrial age. No; we are just on the threshold of * * * "the industrial and comfortable age," and Mr. Hoover will be its first great leader. He is our first example of the new type of Statesman.*—HENRY FORD.

The Republican National Committee,
Washington, D. C., 1928

chimney covers. Democratic promoters turned Al Smith's signature brown derby hat into an instantly recognizable logo on a variety of items.

Many 1928 buttons, issued by independent Protestant activists rather than the Hoover camp, attacked Smith's Catholicism. Many southern Democrats decided to place "Principle Above Party," ignorantly shunning their party's candidate simply to keep the Catholic out of the White House. This created a market for buttons saying, "A Democrat for Hoover," "Anti-Smith," and "A Christian in the White House." (Protestants: Catholics are also Christians.)

A Smith silk pocket handkerchief.

The broom in place of the eraser indicates a "Clean Sweep" for Smith.

A Smith mug.

A miniature featuring Smith's trademark derby.

Smith knee-high stockings.

ABOVE AND RIGHT: Smith license plate attachments.

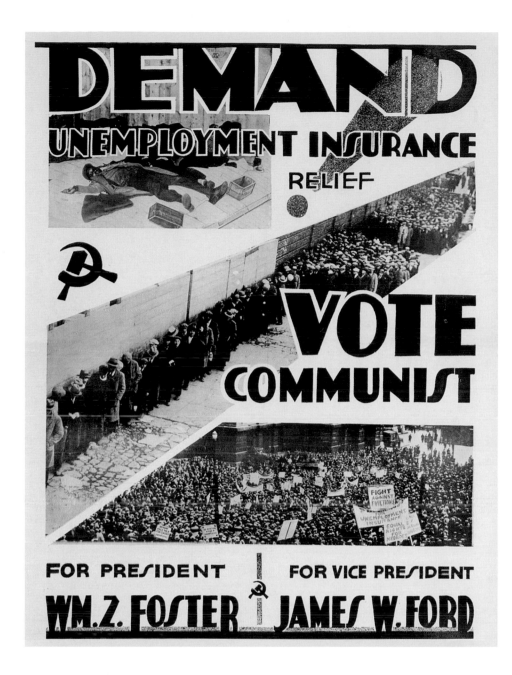

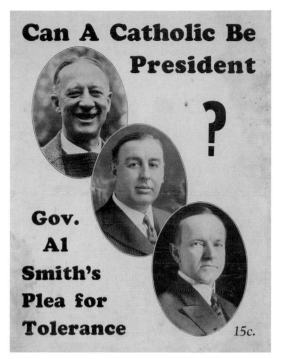

Since there had never been a Catholic president, this brochure tried to win over skeptical voters.

Hoover-Curtis button. Curtis was the first and only candidate who acknowledged that he was half–Native American.

Most Smith campaign items overutilized his terse first name, coating many products with the sayings "I'm for Al," "All for Al," "Me for Al," "We Want Al," and "Good Bye Cal, Hello Al," which sound so delightfully sing-songy when read in succession, don't they? Smitty's "big man on campus" persona gave rise to tapestries and posters proclaiming "America's Biggest Man for America's Biggest Job" and "Happy Warrior," a nickname given to Al by Franklin Roosevelt.

Hoover was a bit shorter on style, so his items stressed his close association with the recent years of Republican prosperity with banners promoting the logical "Four More Years of Prosperity! Why Change?" and "Help Hoover Help Business."

I'd give my shirt for **Roosevelt**

Since the Republicans knew that dismissing Herbert Hoover would mean admitting the Great Depression had been the Republican administration's fault, and because politicians are notoriously loath to ever claim responsibility for any blunder, Hoover won renomination.

The Democrats chose the remarkable Franklin D. Roosevelt, whose perilous bout with polio in 1921 had left him partially paralyzed and confined to a wheelchair. The resilient Roosevelt had fought back to win the governorship in New York, and the hullabaloo surrounding his "new deal for the forgotten man"—a program providing government aid to those struck hardest by the Depression—had won him the presidential nod. Despite his wheelchair, Roosevelt traveled the country delivering more than fifty speeches, including the first in-person acceptance speech at the Democratic convention.

President Hoover insisted that Roosevelt's highfalutin policies were a bunch of bunk, but the poor public craved a way

Roosevelt was the first president to appear on television.

A Hoover license attachment.

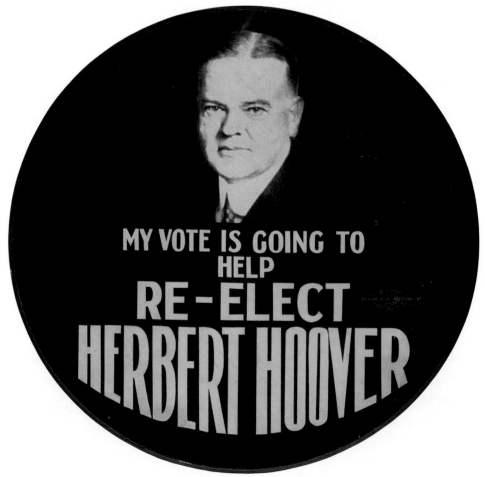

Hoover oil cloth spare tire cover. On early automobile models, spare tires, mounted to the rear or side of the car, were highly visible and served as a prime spot for campaign ads.

HOW ABOUT OUR JOBS?

Governor Roosevelt's proposal to reduce tariffs means:

1. FORCED CLOSING OF MANY AMERICAN FACTORIES.
2. LESS EMPLOYMENT FOR AMERICAN WORKERS.
3. FOREIGN GOODS SWAMPING AMERICAN MARKETS.

Almost all manufacturers in the United States say a reduction in tariffs will hurt their business, according to a recent nation-wide survey made by a non-political organization.

These manufacturers also say if tariffs are reduced they will be forced to lay off large numbers of their employees. Many of them say they will have to close down entirely…they cannot compete against cheap foreign labor.

During October, 172 reporting manufacturers picked at random, said they would be forced to lay off 76,950 workers if tariffs are reduced.

A reduction in the tariff will lessen every worker's chances to find employment or steady work.

Employment is increasing…
Business is improving…
Why rock the boat?

VOTE FOR HOOVER AND KEEP OUR AMERICAN FACTORIES RUNNING

Dlaczego Obywatele Amerykańscy Pochodzenia Polskiego

Powinni wybrać ponownie

HERBERTA HOOVERA

ISSUED BY
REPUBLICAN NATIONAL COMMITTEE
FOREIGN LANGUAGE BUREAU
M. W. TUTHILL, Director

(POLISH)

This Polish Hoover brochure was a version of one created in a variety of languages.

off the breadline and with the New Deal being the best idea in town, Roosevelt snatched forty-two of the forty-eight states.

With the Great Depression in full miserable swing, neither party had the dough to dole out for gaudy regalia. The parties produced more economical items, and most independent manufacturers didn't bother making anything at all.

The Republicans thought that their only chance of victory was to convince the voting public that Roosevelt was a screwball radical, full of nutty notions that would never come to fruition. (Someone who actually talks about fixing the problem instead of tip-toeing away? He must be a loon.) Campaign stamps insisting "Vote for Hoover and Be Safe," as well as license attachments advising "Safe and Sane with Hoover," hinted discretely at Roosevelt's crazy talk while depicting ole reliable Herb as sturdy and free of blame.

In contrast to their pessimistic counterparts, the Democrats jauntily chose "Happy Days Are Here Again" as a campaign anthem. After three straight overwhelming defeats, the Democrats smelled sweet victory with Roosevelt, a

HOO
HOO
HOOVER
FOR
PRESIDENT

DON'T
SWAP
HORSES
★ ★ ★ ★ ★
STAND BY
HOOVER

THIS IS A HOOVER HOUSE
SERVICE - ACHIEVEMENT - VISION
• INTEGRITY •
WOMEN'S COMMITTEE
for
HOOVER

HELP
HOOVER
HELP
BUSINESS

A somewhat primitive Roosevelt light box.

LEFT: A typical Roosevelt poster. Notice that his wheelchair is omitted.

ABOVE: A Roosevelt necktie.

Bring Back **PROSPERITY** *with a* **REPUBLICAN VOTE**

CHEER UP!
THE WORST IS OVER
—
Only a few more months of HOOVER

PAID POLITICAL ADVERTISEMENT

A Franklin Roosevelt mate to this item features the donkey kicking the elephant.

ROOSEVELT GARNER

A Roosevelt license attachment.

candidate who spoke not merely of survival but of a "rendezvous with destiny." His family name didn't hurt either, leading to buttons announcing "America Calls Another Roosevelt, Franklin D."

This Democratic freewheeling exuberance shone through in items featuring caricatures of the Democratic donkey as the "Depression Buster," kicking away hard times (commonly personified by the Republican elephant). The Democrats furthered their rebellious ways by calling for an end to the "noble experiment" of Prohibition. Arm bands insisted "Repeal & Roosevelt," and distinctive license attachments featured Roosevelt, running mate John Nance Garner, and a foaming stein of beer (my kind of president). FDR's main campaign group, "The Friends of Franklin Roosevelt," gave out an estimated nine million free buttons, making sure that every last downtrodden Depression victim found a friend in Roosevelt.

ABOVE: Following Eugene V. Debs's death in 1926, Norman Thomas became the Socialist standard-bearer and was the party's presidential nominee in every election from 1928 to 1948.

A Landon license attachment featuring the Kansan sunflower.

"There is a mysterious cycle in human events. To some generations much is given. Of other generations much is expected. This generation of Americans has a rendezvous with destiny." With his 1932 acceptance speech, Franklin Roosevelt inspired the nation and with his New Deal tactics, made the Democrats the official party of the average Joe. With most Americans seeing the Republicans as haughty rich snoots, the Democrats enjoyed the support of all blue-collar workers, and African-Americans jumped ship from the party of Lincoln for the first time.

Roosevelt's Republican opponent, Kansas governor Alfred M. Landon, combated the New Deal, claiming it pampered its beneficiaries and undermined Americans' individualism. (Blatantly insulting the working class. Doesn't seem like the best election strategy.)

A poll conducted by *Literary Digest*, using names taken at random from telephone books, predicted that Landon would win in a landslide. However, on Election Day, Roosevelt pummeled the Kansas governor by more than ten million votes in one of the worst defeats ever suffered by the nominee of a major party. What happened? The Digesters didn't take into account that during the Depression, many homes could not afford telephones. The only people with phones would be rich Republicans voting for Landon.

By 1936, the public opinion of Roosevelt had polarized into two camps: those who abhorred his maniacal spending and those who anointed him as savior.

ABOVE: A New Deal mug.

RIGHT: A mirror on the reverse side of this plastic sign revealed who really pays for the New Deal.

OPPOSITE: A one-of-a-kind Roosevelt needlepoint.

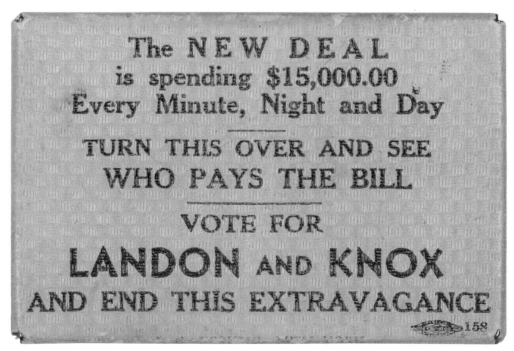

The NEW DEAL is spending $15,000.00 Every Minute, Night and Day

TURN THIS OVER AND SEE WHO PAYS THE BILL

VOTE FOR LANDON AND KNOX AND END THIS EXTRAVAGANCE

ABOVE: A Landon license attachment featuring the Kansan sunflower.

CENTER: A paper napkin detailing Landon's platform.

OPPOSITE: A Landon paper campaign cape.

Luckily for FDR, the second group's numbers greatly outweighed the first, but it did lead to Landon bashing his competitor with stickers saying "Farewell to Alms" and "Willful Waste Makes Woeful Want."

When Landon's campaign wasn't taking shadowboxing swings at FDR, it celebrated his Kansan heritage. Never before had a candidate's home state loomed so large as a theme in his promotion material. The question was why,

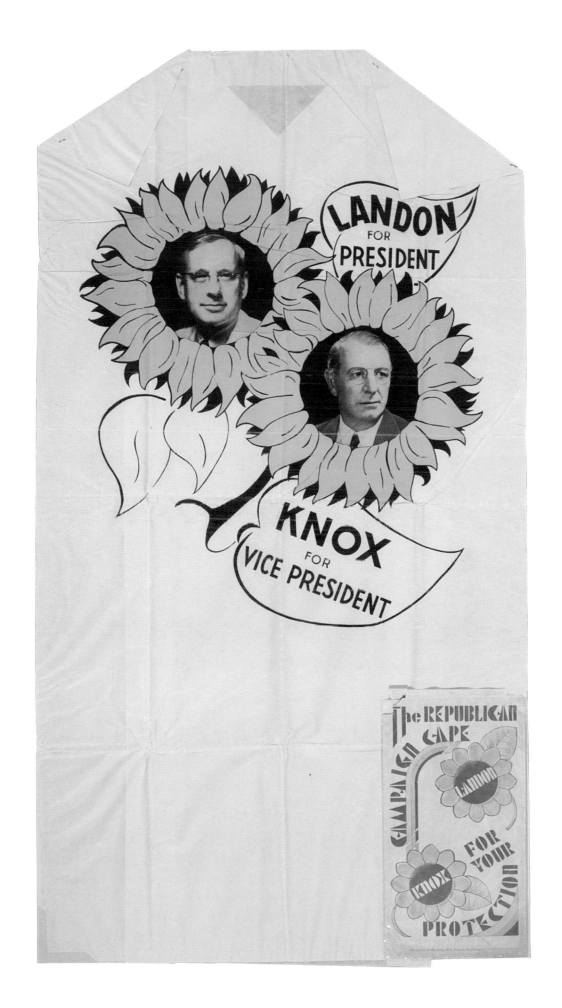

ABOVE: A Landon banner hung at the Republican convention..

RIGHT: This Roosevelt banner hung at the Democratic convention.

Roosevelt's terrier, Fala, had his own brooch.

ABOVE: A Roosevelt spare tire cover.

OPPOSITE: Franklin and Eleanor china dolls.

considering the minuscule number of electoral votes belonging to Kansas. The Landon campaign slapped its logo, the Kansas sunflower, on nearly half of its myriad items.

A few Roosevelt stickers and buttons returned fire on Landon with one rhyming "Back on the Rocks with Landon and Knox" and another playfully sporting a sunflower design and the legend "We Can't Eat Sunflowers/Lose with Landon."

For the most part, however, Roosevelt didn't need to engage in petty word wars. The president had rescued the country from the depths of economic collapse, and was surfing at the crest of an unparalleled wave of popularity. Stickers depicted his metamorphosis from "The People's Champion and Hope" in '32 to "Their Proven Friend and Humane Leader" in '36. Buttons, posters, and banners identified him as "A Gallant Leader" and "Man of the Hour." His New Deal inspired a new trend in campaigning by receiving endorsement items

ALF M. LANDON
Republican Nominee for President

"That leadership along the trail
Which we have loved long since,
And lost awhile,
Has come to us again"

A Landon fan. No air conditioning at stuffy party conventions led to high fan demand throughout the mid-twentieth century.

made by the United Mine Workers, breaking the previous standard of all labor organizations maintaining neutrality. To most Americans, Roosevelt could do no wrong, and if he's good enough for everyone else, then "FDR Is Good Enough for Me."

The image of Alfred E. Newman was created more than thirty years before *Mad* magazine adopted him as a mascot and gave him his name. Originally, anti-Roosevelt ads used him to demonstrate the obliviousness of Roosevelt's supporters.

Copyright applied for

Sure I'm a New Dealer
for "just the two of us" are indispensible

Sure - I'm for Roosevelt

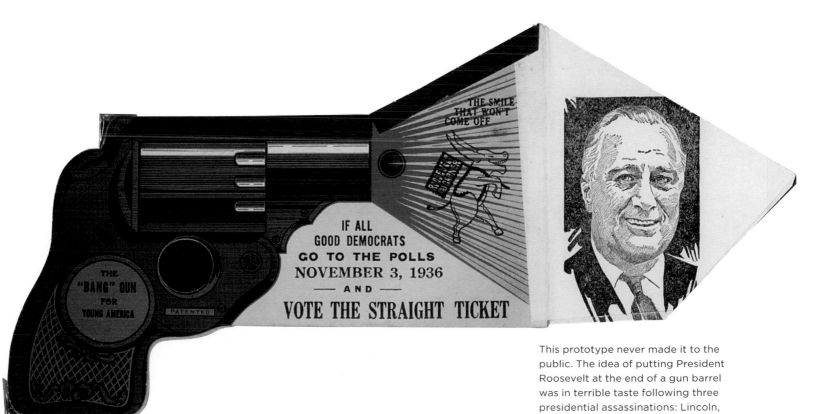

THE SMILE THAT WON'T COME OFF

IF ALL GOOD DEMOCRATS GO TO THE POLLS NOVEMBER 3, 1936 — AND — **VOTE THE STRAIGHT TICKET**

THE "BANG" GUN FOR YOUNG AMERICA

PATENTED

This prototype never made it to the public. The idea of putting President Roosevelt at the end of a gun barrel was in terrible taste following three presidential assassinations: Lincoln, Garfield, and McKinley.

Roosevelt approached his next campaign like a sly boy courting a girl. Just act like you don't want her, and she's all yours. No president had ever run for a third term, and he kept his intentions hush-hush in fear that voters would think him arrogant. When Postmaster General James Farley, a trusted political ally, asked Roosevelt's permission to launch his own campaign, the president shrugged and told him to go ahead. The Democratic Convention then drafted FDR, making it seem as if he was simply bowing to the will of the people.

The Republican nominee, Indiana businessman Wendell L. Willkie, had been a Democrat as late as 1932, and contributed his hard-earned cash to Roosevelt's first campaign. He later flipped to Republican, harboring a personal vendetta against the president after FDR's monopolizing Tennessee Valley Authority hung Willkie's own power company out to dry.

Economic issues slid to the back burner in favor of the burgeoning war in Europe and Roosevelt's potential third term. Both candidates pledged to keep the country out of the war, but those who wanted a strong stand against Hitler chose Roosevelt. Willkie walloped the president for defying the two-term tradition, but given the dangerous international situation, the country decided to stick with a proven, trusted leader.

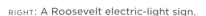

Roosevelt's initials were used to identify him for the first time in 1940.

RIGHT: A Roosevelt electric-light sign.

OPPOSITE: A Roosevelt clock. Notice the subtle anti-Prohibition appeal on the clock face.

ROOSEVELT

AT THE WHEEL FOR A NEW DEAL

ABOVE: A poster for Roosevelt and Lehman (who was running for governor of New York).

RIGHT: In 1940, Postmaster General James Farley asked FDR if he would be running for a third term. After Roosevelt said no, Farley announced his candidacy. This small poster shows Farley as Roosevelt's successor, though FDR's later announcement of his own candidacy knocked Farley out of the race.

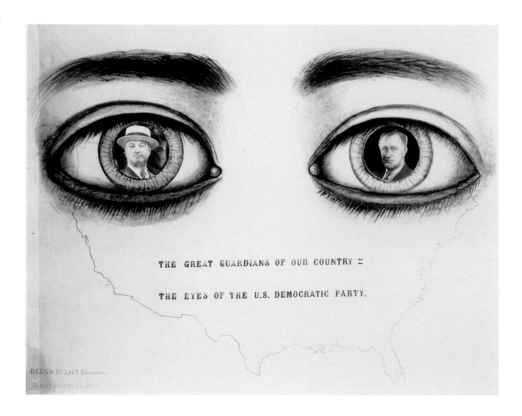

The Army Air Corps Reserve inducted FDR's son, Elliott, in September 1940, at the rank of captain. Almost instantaneously, Republican buttons implying favoritism and nepotism hit the streets, with taunting slogans as "I Wanna Be a Captain Too" and "I Don't Want Elliott for My Captain." Such was the tone of the 1940 election.

After a slight trinketry renaissance in 1936, the 1940 contest between Roosevelt and Republican challenger Wendell Willkie boomed with an estimated fifty-four million buttons ordered between the two campaigns. Chalk up the revival to the remarkable Republican push to put the brakes on a Roosevelt third term. The country had developed a deeply polarized love/hate relationship with their leader, and the Willkie camp provided a poster or button for just about every single dissenter, severely outnumbering Roosevelt regalia in variety and volume.

The Willkie camp took FDR's weak spots and pasted them on every button, stamp, or sticker they could find. The standout outcry was against the third

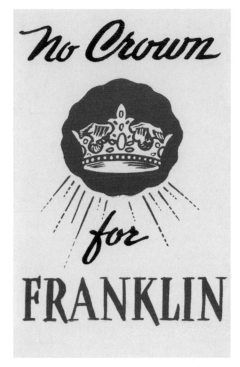

ABOVE: An anti-Roosevelt postcard.

LEFT: Many posters (beginning in this era and continuing until after the war) were aimed at Chinese-Americans.

Re-elect President

F. D. ROOSEVELT
FOR PRESIDENT

MEMBER OF
WILLKIE
FOR PRESIDENT
CLUB

WIN WITH WILLKIE

A plaster Wilkie head to hang on your wall.

A set of "No Third Term" matches.

LEFT, TOP AND BOTTOM: Wilkie plug-in light boxes.

OPPOSITE: Wilkie compared himself to "Honest Abe," opting to paste Lincoln's face all over his stamps rather than his own.

A

PAUPER
FOR
ROOSEVELT

LET'S GIVE
FRANKLIN
UNEMPLOYMENT
INSURANCE

THANKSGIVING
DAY
NOV. 5

Election Returns
WILLKIE 1st
Roosevelt 2nd

NO
MORE
FIRESIDE
CHATS

NO MAN
IS GOOD
THREE
TIMES

ELEANOR
Start Packing
THE WILLKIES
Are Coming

A salesman's pin displaying both candidates.

WE
DON'T WANT
ELEANOR
EITHER

DR. JEKYLL
— of —
HYDE PARK

I'LL BET MY
ON
WILLKIE

100
MILLION
BUTTONS
CAN'T BE
WRONG

OUT!
STEALING
THIRD

IF
I WERE
21
I'D VOTE FOR
WILLKIE

JOE LOUIS
FOR WILLKIE

term. Items bore legends ranging from the cut-and-dry "No Third Term," to "Exterminate Third Termites," to "Strike Three F. D. /You're Out" to the witty sexual analogy "Confucius Say . . . Man Who Stand Up Twice, No Good Third Time." Some items implicated Roosevelt as royalty, reading "Roosevelt for King," "No Roosevelt Dynasty," and "We Want Roosevelt to Abdicate."

Other Willkie items lampooned Roosevelt's record, referring to the New Deal as a "Raw Deal," but the most scathing attacks targeted FDR's personal life. "I Hate Wah" and "Mah Friends, Goodbye" buttons parodied his accent, while "Flash! Deeds Made America, Not Fireside Chats" buttons, mocked his radio talks. The

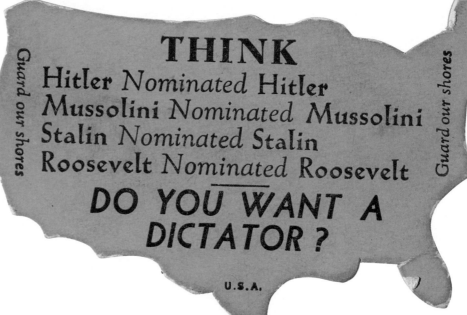

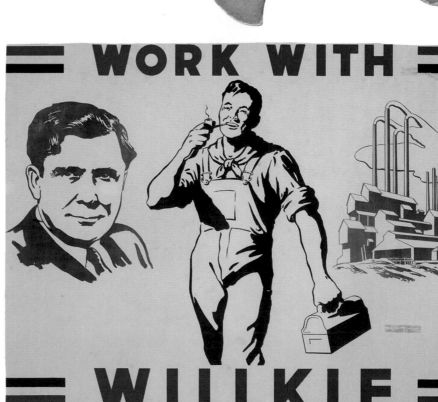

ABOVE: Anti-FDR memorabilia.

RIGHT: This Wilkie poster claimed that Roosevelt had not saved the nation from the Depression.

FOR
PRESIDENT

"He
Chews
to Run"

"He
Talks
Sense"

WILL ROGERS

"The only politician who is funny intentionally"

Read his campaign speeches in LIFE every week

An ad promoting Will Rogers's fake candidacy in *Life* magazine.

Republicans made Eleanor Roosevelt their punching bag as well, satirizing her syndicated newspaper column "My Day" and manufacturing buttons reading "Roosevelt Is Buying the Aquacade to Keep Eleanor Home," which utilized Billy Rose's aquatic revue and its star to ridicule Mrs. Roosevelt's penchant for travel.

The Willkie items put Roosevelt on the defensive, with his buttons (mostly made by commercial vendors) claiming "Better a Third Termer than a Third Rater," and portraying Willkie as the champion of the rich with a "Willkie for the Millionaires/Roosevelt for the Millions" button.

"Wear The Key To Prosperity"

A salesman's card picturing a popular Willkie rebus.

About with polio, twelve years in the White House, a Great Depression, and arguably the most brutal war in human history had taken their toll. Roosevelt's health was understandably failing. The Democratic Party was certain to nominate him for a fourth term, but a few top party leaders had the foresight to assume that Roosevelt would probably die in office, making the choice of his running mate absolutely crucial. Because most of these men disliked the current vice president, Henry A. Wallace (whom they viewed as a Socialist), they booted him, and gave the spot to Senator Harry Truman of Missouri.

The Republican candidate, New York governor Thomas E. Dewey, won on the first convention ballot with an impressive 1,056 of the 1,057 votes. Dewey was a tough cookie; he had earned his stripes fighting the mob as the district attorney in

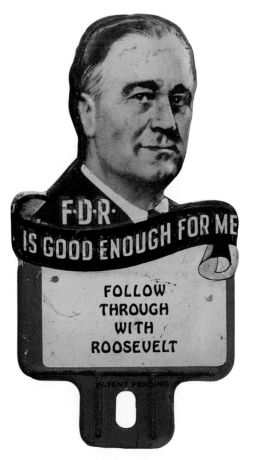

ABOVE: License plate attachment.

RIGHT: A wire metal sculpture of FDR. It is one of a few items that depict the president smoking. The campaign smartly figured that a smiling Roosevelt was more accessible to the public than FDR grimacing while smoking out of his customary gaudy cigarette holder.

Franklin and Eleanor gilt-edged,
Impressionistic coat buttons.

New York City and eliminating corruption in the state's police department, and improved conditions in mental health facilities while governor.

With World War II still going strong, Dewey decided not to touch the issue of foreign policy, instead opting to question Roosevelt's frail health, attacking the "tired old man" in Washington. In response, Roosevelt's doctor announced that the president was fit as a fiddle, and FDR campaigned in harsh weather to prove that he was well enough to lead.

The Democrats argued that Dewey, who had zero foreign policy experience, was unqualified to take the nation's reins during wartime, leading to the Democratic slogan, "Don't Change Horses Midstream." In November, FDR won again, but by a narrower margin than in any of his previous victories.

An FDR pipe.

THE **AVENUE** OF **TOMORROW**

VOTE FOR THE COMMANDER-IN-CHIEF, PRES. ROOSEVELT

WHO STANDS FOR JUSTICE OF ALL THE PEOPLE

Freedom TO EARN *Freedom* TO PRODUCE

U. S. MONUMENTAL HIGHWAY SOCIETY

FOURTEEN MILLION HAPPY WORKERS

THE OLD KENTUCKY NOVELTY NEWS HOUSE · 432 South Main Street, Los Angeles, Calif.

This poster unjustly implied that due to vice presidential nominee Truman's rural Southern background, he would support the Klan.

A Roosevelt license plate attachment.

Roosevelt and Republican Thomas E. Dewey's crop of campaign materials was surprisingly dismal after the banner year of 1940. The drought was especially strong in the Republican camp. Buttons tapped into Dewey's New York City crime-fighting persona, with legends reading "Dewey the Racket Buster/New Deal Buster" and his economic ideas, leading America "Back to Work Quicker with Dewey and Bricker."

Roosevelt items, however, slathered on the patriotic fervor. Buttons bore such sentiments as "Support Your Commander in Chief," "For Freedom/44," and "I Am an American," the last of which is actually more an indication of your citizenship than a candidate endorsement. Some featured the preemptive "V" symbol for victory, while others sought to counteract fourth-term backlash with such slogans as "Three Good Terms Deserve Another," and "Go 4th to Win the War."

A homemade Dewey elephant.

ABOVE: "I'm doing a block for Dewey" meant that you vowed to go door to door to promote his candidacy. That's fine, but why put the block in a jewelry box? I'm sure it resulted in some very disappointed wives.

LEFT: A Dewey apron.

It's a Dewey Day

Vote ⊗ Republican

THOMAS E. DEWEY | EARL WARREN

A Dewey fan distributed at the Republican convention.

N o one thought of Harry Truman as anything more than a political placeholder. First, liberals within the Democratic Party, including FDR's sons, tried to lure retired general Dwight Eisenhower to run as a Democrat, but Dwight declined. Then at the convention, Hubert H. Humphrey of Minneapolis led a successful fight to include a strong civil rights plank in the party platform, causing thirty-five bigoted southern delegates to storm out in protest. How did this affect Truman? Following the convention, the same cranky southern Democrats formed the States' Right (or Dixiecrat) Party, nominating South Carolina governor Strom Thurmond for president. And if that weren't enough, the liberal Roosevelt wing of the party, upset with Truman's steadfast stand against the Soviet Union, re-formed the Progressive Party, putting up Henry Wallace as their candidate.

Truman was the first president to travel underwater in a modern submarine.

With the Democrats morphing into this quarrelling three-headed monster, few people gave Truman a chance to beat Thomas Dewey, again the Republican nominee. But "Give 'em Hell Harry" was not going down without a fight. During a thirty-thousand-mile train campaign, the spunky Truman made 300 speeches to six million people, launching blunt attacks on the "do-nothing Eightieth Congress."

Despite all his rabblerousing, the polls and even the early returns indicated a Dewey victory. The *Chicago Tribune* went

ABOVE: A Dewey pin.

RIGHT: Perhaps the most famous newspaper headline in American history.

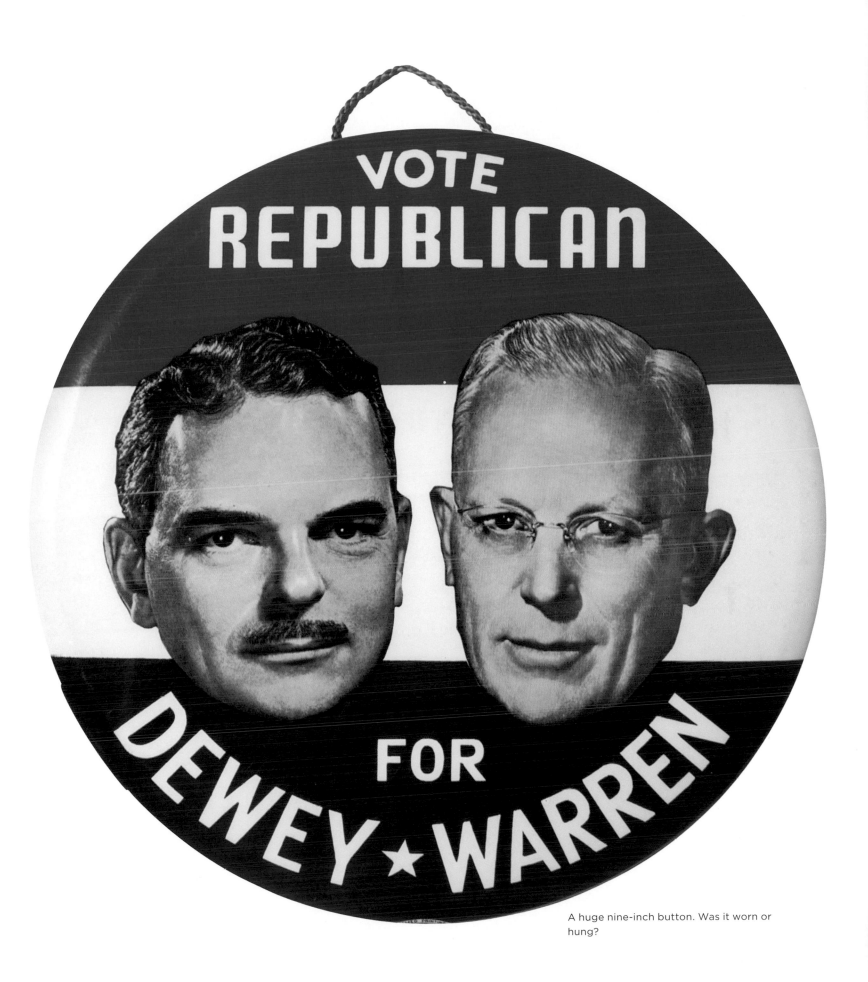

A huge nine-inch button. Was it worn or hung?

LEFT: A Dewey lady's compact.

RIGHT: A three-dimensional Dewey pin.

敬請美籍華人選民
一致擁選杜威華倫

VOTE DEWEY —— WARREN
and Republican Congress

美籍華人擁護杜威華倫競選正副總統委員會
（職員一覽表）

	WILBUR W. H. PYN		
倪卓屏	CHAIRMAN		主
	EXECUTIVE COMMITTEE	財 交 西 中 宣 總	席
伍天生夫人	MRS. ELSIE W. WU	政 際 文 文 傳 務	
黃建章	WELLINGTON HONG ART	主 主 秘 秘 主 主	
陳庭光	EDWARD CHIN	任 任 書 書 任 任	
伍嘉言	DAVID N. K. FEE		
湯鴻業	EDWARD HONG	梅 方 湯 陳 余 盧 倪	
湯鴻業夫人	MRS. MAE SIEN HONG	金 梅 鴻 庭 觀 卓	
方瑞雄夫人	MRS. JOSEPHINE MOY HONG	波 玉 業 光 煥 黎 屏	
盧觀黎	LOO KOON LAI	瓊 夫	
李喜祖	LUN F. LEE	人	
李錫鴻	HENRY LEE		
伍 林	LING YEN LEE		
梅金波	GILBERT MOY		
倪卓屏	WILBUR W. H. PYN		
余 煥	DAN F. YEE		

辦事処··64 Mott Street 婦女新運會
辦事日期··由十月廿四日至十一月二日晚
辦事時間··每日由下午一點至晚入点

A poster from the Chinese Republican
Club in New York's Chinatown.

to press, and the headline "Dewey Defeats Truman" hit newsstands. It ended
up being a huge waste of paper. Truman's upset victories in California and Ohio
clinched his election, and the headline clinched its spot as an all-time great
gaffe.

All the Democratic infighting, along with Dewey's seemingly bottomless
pit of Truman jibes, created a rather handsome batch of 1948 campaign
memorabilia.

"Dixiecrats" Strom Thurmond and Fielding Wright's items dealt with
states' rights, featuring Statue of Liberty posters urging "Get in the Fight
for States' Rights," and another warning "*Now* Is the Time to Fight!" The
uncompromisingly racist and segregationist Thurmond wanted states' rights
simply so that his southern states would have the choice to keep segregation
even if the North abolished it.

The Progressive ticket of Henry Wallace and Glen Taylor swirled in the
complete opposite direction, with "Race Equality/Job Security" stamps and
"Peace/Low Prices/Jobs/Housing/Civil Rights/Repeal Taft-Hartley" cards.
Wallace claimed to be FDR's true reform-minded heir on a button displaying
Wallace's face in front of the familiar FDR silhouette.

Republican campaign items had little to do with Dewey or his platform,
mostly because they were just having too much fun skewering Truman. As one
button insisted, "The Issue Is Truman's Record/Nothing Else!" Others bore such
Truman-socking legends as the tongue-twisting, H-happy "Help Hustle Harry

The sheet music to the campaign theme,
"I'm Just Wild About Harry."

A mechanical cardboard ad for Grogan's Cafe that switches from Truman to Dewey when you pull the tab.

NOBODY WANTS *WAR*

HARRY S. TRUMAN
KNOWS WHY!

TRUMAN
and
BARKLEY

See and Hear...

MR. CIVIL RIGHTS HIMSELF

★

PRESIDENT

HARRY S. TRUMAN

AT THE

Gigantic Registration & Civil Rights Rally

DORRENCE BROOKS SQUARE
136th STREET and ST. NICHOLAS AVENUE

SATURDAY, OCTOBER 11, 1952 at 12 NOON

PRESIDENTIAL ROUTE TO DORRENCE BROOKS SQUARE
Starting time 11:30 A.M. from Lenox Ave. and 110th St., North to 125th St.; West on 125th St. to 7th Ave.; North on 7th Ave. to 155th St.; West on 155th St. to St. Nicholas Ave.; South on St. Nicholas Ave. to 136th St. — DORRENCE BROOKS SQUARE.

REGISTRATION WEEK
MONDAY THROUGH FRIDAY — OCTOBER 6, 7, 8, 9, 10 — 5 P.M. TO 10:30 P.M.
LAST DAY — SATURDAY — OCTOBER 11 — 7 A.M. TO 10:30 P.M.

YOU CANNOT VOTE UNLESS YOU REGISTER

YOU REGISTER NOW AT

POLLING PLACE .... E. D. ....

Your Captain .... Co-Captain ....

★ **NEW YORK COUNTY DEMOCRATIC COMMITTE** ★
CARMINE G. DeSAPIO, Leader

FOR PRESIDENT

HARRY S. TRUMAN

TRUMAN
CIVIL RIGHTS

GET IN THE FIGHT FOR STATES' RIGHTS

STATES' RIGHTS

SHIELD OF YOUR LIBERTY

J. STROM THURMOND
for President

FIELDING L. WRIGHT
for Vice-President

STATES' RIGHTS DEMOCRATS

WALLACE FOR PRESIDENT

ABOVE: Wallace, former vice president under Roosevelt and presidential nominee of the Progressive Party, was perpetually in Roosevelt's shadow.

LEFT: Strom Thurmond represented South Carolina in the U.S. Senate from 1954 to 1964 as a Democrat and from 1964 to 2003 as a Republican. Thurmond also ran for president in 1948 as a member of the prosegregation States' Rights Democratic Party, winning thirty-nine electoral votes.

Home," "I Want a True-Man/Not Harry," and "Start Packing Harry/The Deweys Are Coming." Truman's remodeling of a deck area at the White House provided fuel for another Dewey jibe, "Truman Was Screwy to Build a Porch for Dewey." Possibly the jackass-like tone of the Dewey campaign inspired buttons featuring caricatures of jackasses to help form such slogans as "I'll Bet my (picture of jackass) on Dewey" and "Keep Your (picture of jackass) Off the Grass/It's Dewey."

With the Democrats short on funds due to their dissenters, and independent campaign groups unwilling to link themselves to a certain loser, the Truman campaign inspired far fewer objects than Dewey's. Although Truman's obnoxious tirades fricasseeing the "do-nothing" Republican Congress made his the more vocally negative of the two campaigns, few buttons besides the juvenile yet hilarious "Phooey on Dewey" directly attacked his competitor. The items instead amazingly enough focused on issues (didn't even think of that approach, did you, Dewey?), especially the burgeoning Cold War, including "Secure the Peace" posters and the especially effective "Nobody Wants War/ Harry S. Truman Knows Why" posters, portraying the veteran, Truman, in his gallant World War I captain's uniform. A few buttons bit back at defector Strom Thurmond with the legends "Truman Fights for Human Rights" and "States Rights or Human Rights?"

REPUBLICANS draft

GENERAL MacARTHUR FOR PRESIDENT

In 1952, the Republican Party tried to draft General Douglas MacArthur, who served in both World Wars, as its presidential nominee, but reneged when General Eisenhower agreed to run.

1952–PRESENT

In 1976, Jimmy Carter's media director Gerald Rafshoon decided to finally put the kibosh on giveaway campaign buttons altogether until a chorus of complaints from local Carter-Mondale headquarters caused him to reconsider, simply because "it wasn't worth it to have the complaints." He begrudgingly ordered up two hundred thousand inexpensive lithographed tin buttons, roughly one for every volunteer, to shut them up. Rafshoon explained, "Who wears buttons? It's the people who work in the headquarters of operations. If you send them enough for themselves, they'll have them and that's that. This is to placate campaign workers." Call him a shrewd businessman or tightwad, but Rafshoon knew the political climate. By 1976, buttons weren't used to sway votes, only as keepsakes for party activists at conventions and caucuses.

Though the era between 1952 and 1972 yielded perhaps the most creative crop of items yet, campaigners found little use for them.

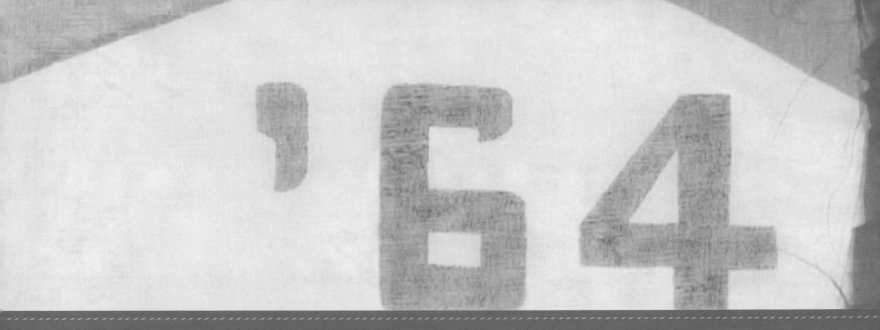

'64

Presidential campaigns had evolved into meticulously staged media events, with Movietone News and radio giving way to the monster of television. You can't hand people buttons while they're home on the couch. Televised debates, press conferences, and commercials became a much more effective way for candidates to reach the largest possible chunk of the voting public. With my collection focusing on tangible objects, I won't be directly touching upon TV spots.

Local antilitter laws doomed most telephone- and power-pole papers, and rousing rounds of political Doorbell Dixies diminished, with doorknob hangers dying out. The items that weathered the storm adjusted to the times. Straight pinbacks on buttons easily sliced through the new, all-the-rage double-knit sweaters, inadvertently piercing chests. Answer: Buttons with safety pin and lockpin fasteners, along with cheap rolls of lapel stickers first introduced in 1968 with the cheeky sticker, "If I Had a Button, It

Would Say Humphrey-Muskie." The advent of stickers for your bumper bumped the previous auto champ, license attachments, to the discount rack. Beginning in 1956, bumper stickers provided the perfect balance between highly visible candidate endorsement and anonymity for the bashful motorist, and became the most significant single avenue of personal political expression, even though they were impossible to peel off. For months after the election, citizens would groggily walk to their vehicles every morning, and say "Dammit, I need to get that loser Stevenson off my bumper," until the not-quite-as-sticky vinyl stickers of the '70s alleviated the problem.

While some items were tailored for a reserved public, celluloid buttons let it all hang out with festive bright colors and gaudy sizes. Candidates and their party supporters donned massive buttons (up to nine inches in diameter), with their silliness easily visible to television audiences. "Flasher" buttons refracted light, allowing

1   2   3

one to see alternating designs from different vantage points. Many campaign boutiques sold buttons depicting candidates with toy-like googly eyes.

And these celluloids were only the tip of the eclectic iceberg. Nineteen-fifty-two nylon stockings proclaiming "I Like Ike" and "I'm Madly for Adlai" promoted their candidates, but did not exactly break new ground in feminine fashion. Garish plastic "Don't Be Static, Vote Democratic" and "I Like Ike" sunglasses appeared in 1956, blocking sun and style simultaneously. Campaign cosmetics included "I Like Ike" hand lotion packets and deodorant soap promising Goldwater partisans "4-Year Protection." Novelty food and drink included 1960 Richard Nixon and John Kennedy ice cream bars (leading voters to choose their candidate based on which one tastes better. Mmm . . . this Nixon is so delicious. He has my vote!) and 1964 soft drinks "Gold Water" and "Johnson Juice" (I'm not even going to touch those two).

4   5   6

"Let's face it. The only excuse for Ike's candidacy is that he's the man best qualified to deal with Stalin," one Republican strategist said. Both parties had been trying fruitlessly for years to court World War II hero Dwight D. Eisenhower, until Ike finally gave in to the Republicans and their strong national defense platform. With Ike in tow, and anticommunist crusader Richard M. Nixon of California as his running mate, the Republicans' military might was ready to correct the Democratic policy of pussyfooting around the Reds.

Eisenhower's Democratic opponent, Adlai E. Stevenson, perpetuated the timid reputation; most of the public viewed the eloquent Illinois governor as an overbearing egghead.

The Eisenhower campaign proceeded without a hitch until the *New York Times* reported that Nixon had used campaign contributions to create a "slush" fund, out of which he had paid some of his personal expenses. With a peeved Eisenhower threatening to drop him from the ticket, Nixon went on national television to talk himself out of the hole. In his now famous September 23 "Checkers" speech, he denied the report but did admit to receiving one gift: a cocker spaniel named Checkers. "Regardless of what they say about it," Nixon declared, "we're going to keep it." (Aw, puppies! I can't stay mad at Nixon, he likes puppies!) Neither could America. Eisenhower-Nixon in a landslide.

ABOVE: Delegates sipped this drink at the Republican convention.

BELOW: This soap's slogan was both literal and figurative following the scandals of the Truman administration.

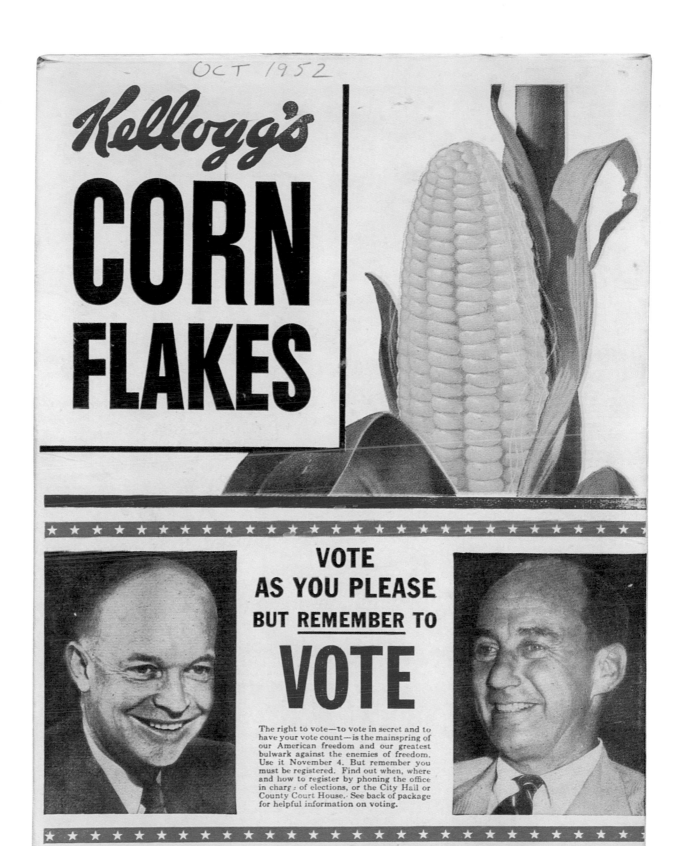

This corn flakes box promotes voting in the 1952 election.

This Eisenhower banner hung at the Republican convention.

David Eisenhower gave me this shirt, which he wore during his grandfather's campaign.

The 1952 and 1956 campaigns of Dwight Eisenhower and Adlai Stevenson produced arguably the most successful catch phrase in American history, the unmistakable "I Like Ike." Though many successful marketing slogans pound us every day, people's preference for Ike was the first inescapable modern media slogan. "I Wanna Be Like Mike," for one, followed a very similar pattern, and perhaps "Yo Quiero Taco Bell" took its cue from the multilingual outreach of "Yo Quiero Ike," "J'Aime Ike," "Mi Piace Ike," and "Me Gusta Ike," with other items featuring the slogan in Morse code, sign language, and Braille.

Very few Eisenhower items were issue-oriented in either campaign, focusing mostly on portraying Ike as a strong, trustworthy leader. Buttons insisted "Eisenhower Will Guard My Future" and " Keep America Strong with

Carved wooden bottle stoppers for Eisenhower and MacArthur produced while both were deciding whether to enter the 1952 presidential contest.

This Eisenhower head stores your sewing needles.

"I Like Ike" socks.

ADLAI STEVENSON

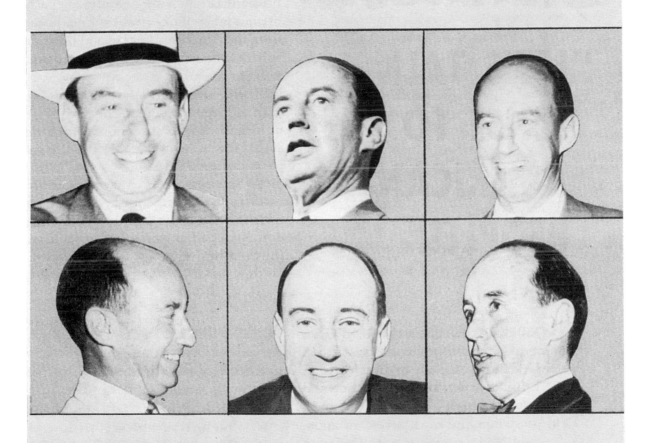

FACES THE FUTURE

ABOVE: Stevenson and Kefauver pot holders.

RIGHT: A Kefauver tab. Tennessee Senator Kefauver was often pictured wearing a coonskin cap à la his state's most famous citizen, Davy Crockett.

Ike." Some items were just plain silly. Nineteen-fifty-two "Time for a Change" buttons featured babies in diapers, and the 1956 convention "We're Fore Ike" packages of golf tees hinted at Eisenhower's celebrated preference for the fairways over the Oval Office.

Stevenson's campaign coated trinkets with all sorts of hilariously sorry catchphrases in a futile attempt to match his competitor. The extensive list included "I Say Adlai," "Madly for Adlai," "We Need Adlai Badly," "OK with Adlai," "I Like Adlai," "We Believe in Steve," even "Adlai and Estes Are the Bestes'," all of which belly-flopped in the looming shadow of "I Like Ike."

A Kefauver whistle.

A brochure.

An Eisenhower compact with a rotary phone design.

America just can't seem to keep those presidents healthy. In 1955, Eisenhower suffered what his doctors called a "moderate" heart attack, and in 1956, he had undergone serious intestinal surgery. Nevertheless, the Republicans backed him for another term.

As for the Democrats, Adlai Stevenson had clawed his way back to the top of the party after Ike stomped on him four years earlier, and he won his second straight nomination, taking Tennessee senator Estes Kefauver as his running mate over Massachusetts senator John F. Kennedy.

Aside from the heart attack, Eisenhower was doing a bang-up job. He had stuck a fork in the Korean War, as promised, and had given the Soviet Union a piece of his mind (Khrushchev was not exactly chanting "I Like Ike"). At

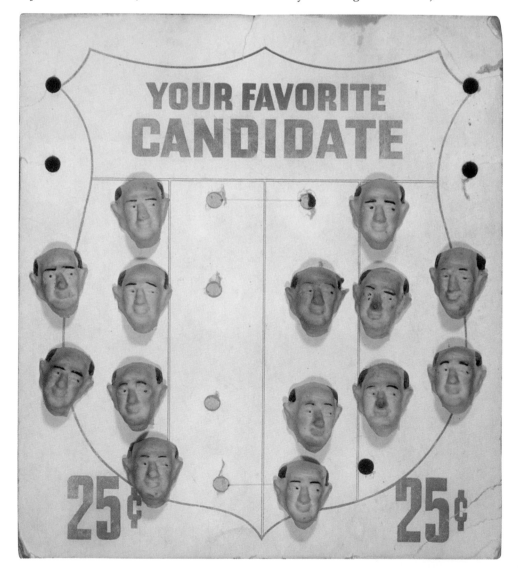

YOUR FAVORITE CANDIDATE

25¢   25¢

A salesman's card of lapel pins featuring a rubber head of the candidate.

"I Like Ike" buttons in assorted languages.

ABOVE, TOP: Eisenhower lady's gloves.

LEFT: Stevenson stockings.

ABOVE, CENTER: A plastic beanie with an elephant whose head bobs up and down.

ABOVE, RIGHT: A pair of Eisenhower suspenders.

ABOVE: Eisenhower and Nixon pot holder.

LEFT: Stevenson and Eisenhower popcorn was sold at movie theaters around the country as the election drew closer. The company that produced the boxes used its sales data to predict that Stevenson would win the election. I guess all those Eisenhower voters just didn't like popcorn.

BELOW: A Stevenson bubble gum cigar box.

home, employment was up, and people felt prosperous. The only issue that the Democrats could use was Eisenhower's health, and that was not nearly enough, with the public electing Eisenhower and Nixon easily, by two million more votes and two more states than they had last time. The president's popularity didn't seem to extend to his Republican brethren. Both the House and the Senate remained Democratic. It was the first time since Zachary Taylor won in 1848 that a victorious presidential candidate failed to carry a single house of Congress for his party.

TOP: When a famous photo caught Stevenson with a hole in his shoe, the Eisenhower campaign jumped at the chance to show him as meager and broke.

BOTTOM: The Stevenson campaign approached the holey shoe in their own way: Stevenson is working so hard for you that he's wearing his shoes out.

Matching cigarettes and sunglasses for Eisenhower and Stevenson voters. Although campaigns had distributed many pipes over the years, this was the first time cigarettes promoted candidates.

A noise-maker toy.

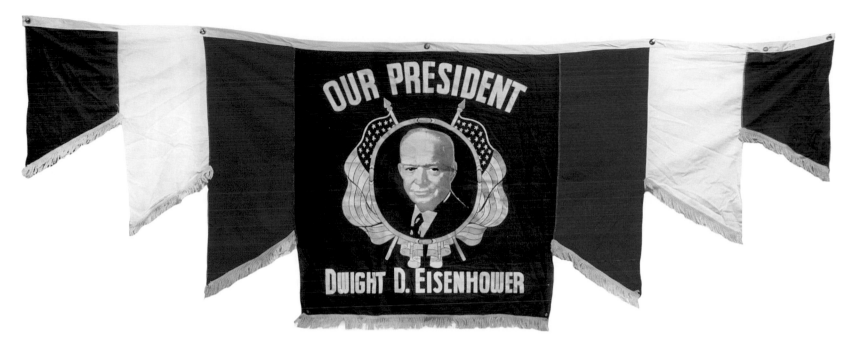

America's First Lady
JAQUELINE KENNEDY

1960: **All the Way with JFK**

Democrat John F. Kennedy had the odds stacked against him. Americans liked their Ike, so most insiders assumed that vice president Richard Milhous Nixon was a shoe-in to take over. Also, Kennedy was Catholic, and Democrats feared that he would suffer the same poundings and persecution as Al Smith in 1928. But Kennedy was no Al Smith. He was a handsome born charmer and his early victory in the West Virginia primary proved that Kennedy could win in a heavily Protestant state.

> Kennedy was (and remains) the only president to have won the Pulitzer Prize, for his book *Profiles in Courage*.

The race remained tight as the debates approached. Over one hundred million Americans tuned in to watch the first-ever nationally televised debate. Though both men spoke eloquently, Kennedy's youthful vibrancy and sassy smiles trumped the pale Nixon who had recently been hospitalized, carrying Kennedy to a narrow victory six weeks later.

Although John Kennedy took home the prize in 1960, his campaign items lacked firepower, overlooking a slew of possibilities. No items referenced his popular *Profiles in Courage* book, only one shamrock button played upon his Irish lineage, and no mention was made of his opponent "Tricky Dick"'s tendency toward scandal.

"A PROFILE IN COURAGE"

ELECT U. S. SENATOR
JOHN F. KENNEDY
VICE PRESIDENT

This button was produced for the 1956 convention when John F. Kennedy sought the vice presidential nomination on Adlai E. Stevenson's ticket.

Franklin Roosevelt's New Deal
John Kennedy's New Frontier

IN THE 1960's AS IN THE 1930's
THE TIMES CALL FOR LEADERSHIP

A UAW CITIZENSHIP EDUCATION POSTER

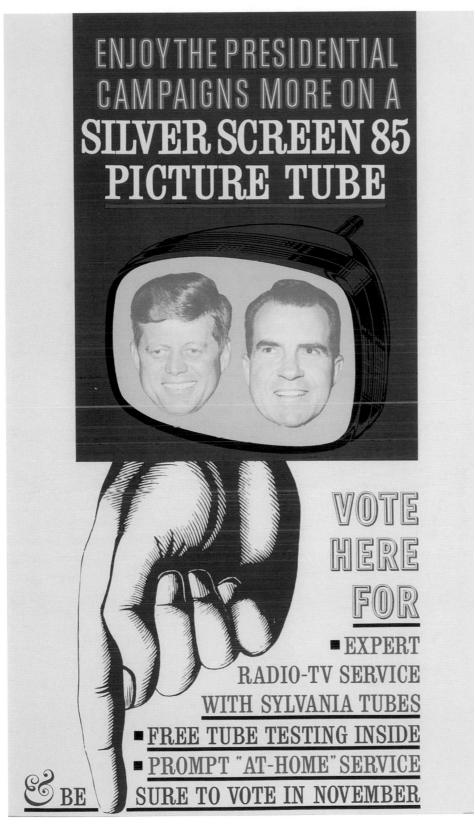

If you wanted to see the Kennedy/Nixon debates, you needed a television with a Silver Screen Picture Tube.

Similar to the Eisenhower/Stevenson popcorn battle in 1956, Good Humor launched a line of Kennedy and Nixon ice cream bars. Nixon bars outsold Kennedy's overwhelmingly. (How many children would even care which candidate graced their ice cream wrapper?)

THE FIRST FAMILY BRACELET

An usher sported this cloth vest and paper hat at the Democratic convention.

KENNEDY FOR PRESIDENT

When torpedoes sank Kennedy's PT109 naval ship near Japan during World War II, Kennedy rescued some of his shipmates. These heroics were the perfect inspiration for memorabilia.

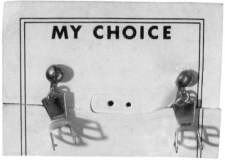

MY CHOICE

Due to back trouble, President Kennedy regularly sat in a rocking chair, inspiring these earrings.

A Kennedy cork bottle-stopper.

Kennedy rocking-chair salt and pepper shaker.

Instead, Kennedy buttons tried in vain, as candidates would in most subsequent elections, to create his own "I Like Ike." The campaign's favorites were "Let's Back Jack" and "All the way with JFK," but other efforts included "I'm Gone for John," and "Kennedy is the Remedy." Flashers, posters, and bumper stickers echoed Kennedy's pledge "to get America moving again," and to lead the public to "The New Frontier." PT-109 lapel pins celebrated Kennedy's renown as a World War II naval hero.

Unlike the Kennedy campaign, the Nixon effort never hesitated to sling mud. It satirized Kennedy's youth with "Don't Send a Boy" brochures, along with "Nix-on Kennedy" and "Don't Be a *Jack*-Ass, Vote Republican" buttons.

Nixon's "I Like Ike" attempts included "My Pick is Dick," "Click with Dick," and "Nixon Now." A major challenge of the Nixon campaign buttons was to make their Dick likeable, some by focusing on his popular wife with slogans

EXCLUSIVE! **PAT NIXON**

TELLS THE PROBLEMS OF A CANDIDATE'S WIFE

IN NOVEMBER

LADIES' HOME

JOURNAL

PRINTED IN U.S.A. 11-62

Fake money implying that profligate
Kennedy was oblivious to the national debt.

The Theocratic Party was the first to
base its platform completely on Christian
beliefs.

A Nixon elephant
bobble head.

like "Pat for First Lady" and "We want Pat, Too," while also showing Nixon's lighter side in "They Can't Lick Our Dick." Nixon's most successful slogan was "Experience Counts," playing upon his eight years of vice presidency versus the comparatively green Kennedy. And perhaps even funnier than the "Dick" jokes were the 1960 items portraying Nixon as a man of sterling personal virtues (made extraordinarily ironic in light of subsequent developments), my favorite being tokens and pins saying simply "Integrity."

Some buttons displayed distaste for both camps, including "Prostitutes: Vote for Kennedy or Nixon We Don't Care Who Gets In!" Also, a number of items were produced to promote the last minute third-time candidacy of perennial loser Adlai Stevenson with slogans like "I'm *Still* Madly for Adlai," the just plain sad "2 Strikes Are Not Out," and "We Can't Afford A Lesser Man."

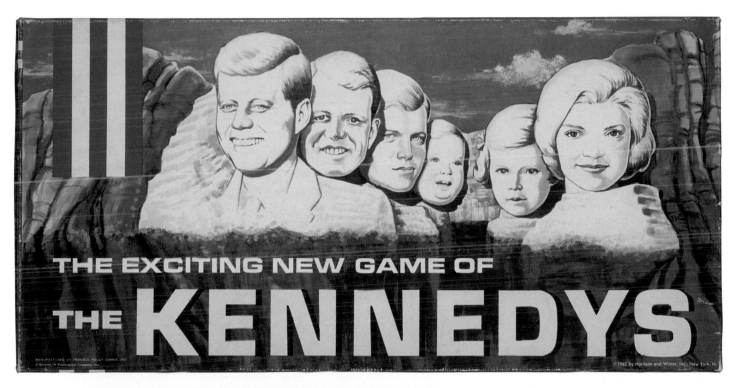

This license plate attachment was made prior to Kennedy's assassination.

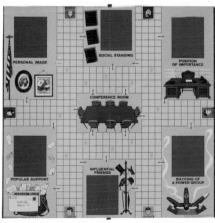

This Clue-style board game features the whole Kennedy family.

CALIFORNIA AU-H₂O

1964: **Gold Water: The Right Drink**

In the short time since JFK's death, Lyndon Johnson had won over the American people as well as the leaders of his party, and had no trouble nabbing the top spot on the Democratic ticket.

Johnson was the first president sworn in by a woman, Federal Judge Sarah T. Hughes.

To take on LBJ, the Republicans picked Senator Barry Goldwater, an extremely conservative Arizonan, whose policies frightened many Americans. Goldwater's harebrained ideas included opposition to civil rights laws and the desire to make Social Security contributions voluntary (a policy that could have very easily led to the first senior citizen riot).

However, it was Goldwater's off-the-wall stance on nuclear war that hurt him the most. He came across to the public as pronuclear fanatic, eager to fling around bombs like Frisbees. Satirists switched Goldwater's "In Your Heart, You Know He's Right" slogan to "In Your Heart, You Know He Might."

Predictably, Goldwater flopped on Election Day. Johnson's strong stand on civil rights hurt him in the South, but nearly everywhere else, Americans turned out for LBJ in overwhelming numbers.

A Goldwater bolo tie in the shape of his home state, Arizona.

SENATOR **Margaret Chase SMITH** for PRESIDENT ☒ VOTE REPUBLICAN

ABOVE: Margaret Chase Smith was the first woman to be elected to both the U.S. House and the Senate, as well as the first to seek a presidential nomination from a major party (she lost to Barry Goldwater).

RIGHT: A Goldwater seat pad intended to keep you comfy at conventions and rallies.

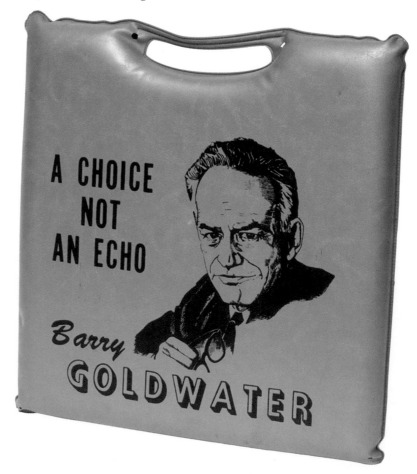

A CHOICE NOT AN ECHO

Barry GOLDWATER

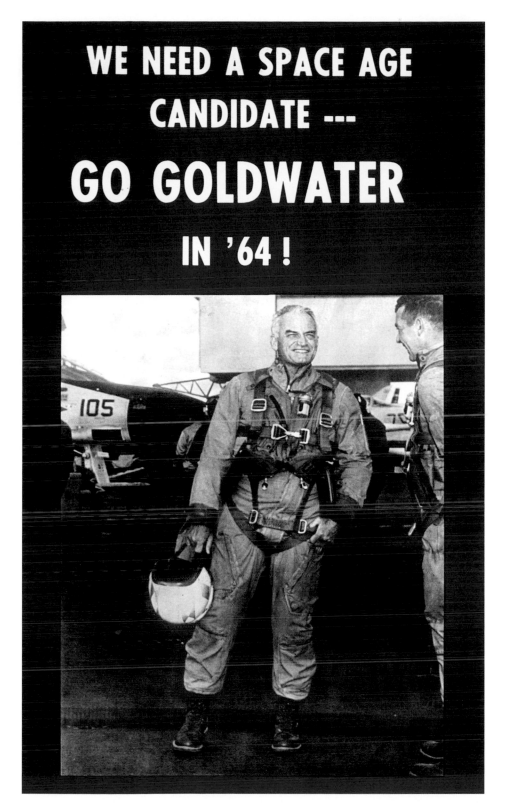

WE NEED A SPACE AGE CANDIDATE ---
GO GOLDWATER
IN '64!

GOLDWATER & MILLER

PANIC BUTTON

A Goldwater panic button pin, inspired by his willingness to bomb Russia.

IN YOUR HEART YOU KNOW HE'S RIGHT

In Barry Goldwater's nomination acceptance speech, he mentioned casually and controversially that "extremism in the defense of liberty is no vice," which, in a way, set the tone for the campaign that followed. Extreme buttons. Extreme t-shirts (for the first time). Extreme soda. Extreme body soap. Goldwater had a different view of politics. Instead of the normal political strategy of riding the moderate line to please everyone for the sake of votes, Goldwater defied

Goldwater's penchant for flying led to his nickname, the Space Age Candidate. As a senator, he was instrumental in helping to create the Air and Space Museum in Washington, D.C.

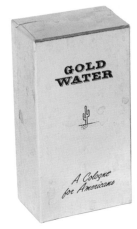

Goldwater cologne and aftershave.

An unsightly Goldwater doll.

A Goldwater mask sported by supporters at the Republican convention.

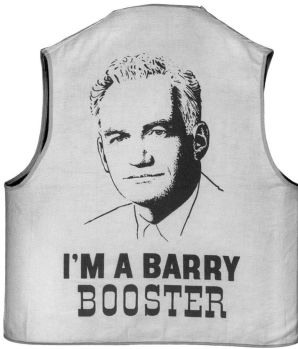

ABOVE: A Goldwater vest worn by a delegate at the Republican convention.

RIGHT: A Goldwater apron.

LEFT: A "Gold Water" six-pack.

RIGHT: "Johnson Juice," the counter to "Gold Water."

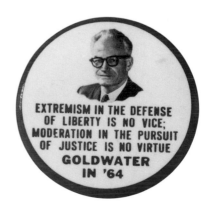

Every Goldwater campaign headquarters had a bowl of this taffy.

conventional wisdom by openly flaunting his angry conservatism. His extreme approach led to such slogans as "I am Extremely Fond of Barry," "I am a Right Wing Extremist," and "I'm an Extremist I Love Liberty." Cans of Gold Water promoted the soda as "The Right Drink for the Conservative Taste" and wrappers on Gold Water soap (which allowed you to wash your extremities with extremism) read "The Soap for Conservative People, 4-Year Protection."

Goldwater's horn-rim glasses (a fashion accessory he stole from Clark Kent) inspired many varieties of jewelry and fold-out wall hangers. His years as a jet pilot gave way to buttons with airplane designs and a poster featuring Goldwater in a flight suit with the slogan "We Need a Space Age Candidate." And no campaign has ever exploited and abused their candidate's name like the Republicans did with "Goldwater" in 1964. They slathered items in metallic gold and created the semiblasphemous "In Gold We Trust" and "Gold for Goldwater" buttons. Others featured glasses of golden water or bubbles with gold particles. Further items promoted the Republican as "AuH_2O," the chemical formula for gold water.

The Goldwater campaign cleverly laid into Johnson as well, with buttons claiming that Johnson's Great Society agenda gave the public "A New Leech on Life." They took a shot at Johnson's wife, Lady Bird, and her beautification project with buttons jibing "Keep America Beautiful: Hide Lady Bird." Johnson's decision to cut back on White House lighting and promote energy efficiency led to "Light Bulb Johnson, Turn Him Out in November."

Battling back against the extreme Goldwater was far too easy. Johnson's campaign changed Goldwater's slogan to "In Your Guts You Know He's Nuts" and switched around the Goldwater chemistry to "AuH_2O: Fool's Gold" and "$C_5H_4N_4O_3$ on AuH_2O," which meant uric acid on gold water. (Far too much chemistry, guys.) Democrats skewered Goldwater's nuclear-happy ways with buttons featuring mushroom clouds and linking Goldwater to the title character in the Cold War farce *Dr. Stangelove*, calling him "Dr. Strangewater."

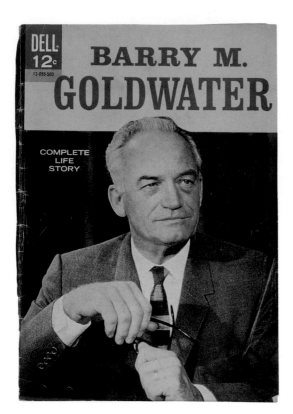

ABOVE, LEFT: An *Archie*-style comic book telling the story of Goldwater's life.

ABOVE, RIGHT: A poster featuring the chemical formula version of Goldwater's name.

RIGHT: A Goldwater game.

An impartial pin.

A piece of Johnson jewelry.

A Johnson Stetson hat worn at the Democratic convention.

BELOW, LEFT AND RIGHT: Goldwater and Johnson posters appealing to Chinese-Americans.

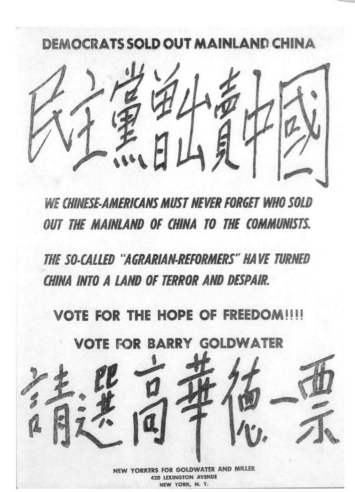

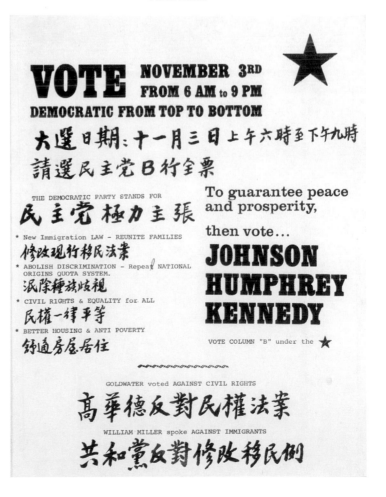

LYNDON B. JOHNSON

A large Johnson ceramic tile.

A classic Johnson poster.

Johnson's items were less "extreme" than Goldwater's, and kept to mundane slogans such as "All the Way with LBJ" and "USA Likes LBJ" for flashers and tie clips, among other items. Many buttons and tabs focused on Johnson's Texan identity, with cowboy boots and spurs making over the president into a regular John Wayne. Especially popular were buttons reading "Let Us Continue," in conjunction with Johnson's pledge to continue the unfinished work of President Kennedy. Some Kennedy 1964 campaign regalia was already under production before his death, with buttons reading "Jack/Once More in '64," and "I Want Jack Back" having to be sadly shelved.

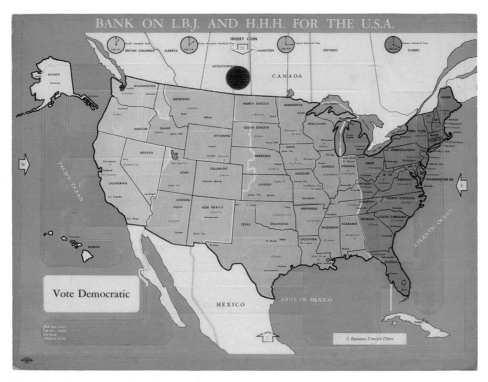

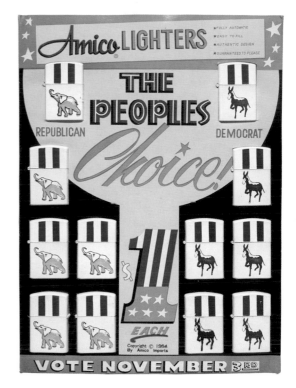

You play this game by dropping a coin between the plastic walls and then shifting the board, allowing the coin to move through the maze.

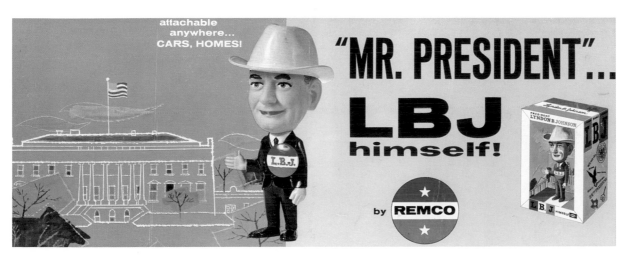

I saw these goofy dashboard dolls at a cowboy store in Arizona. There was a huge display, and I bought the whole thing.

A Republican elephant produced in India.

"FORE" NIXON
PUTTING MARKER

When Lyndon Johnson opted not to run for reelection, Democrats scrambled to snatch the nomination, including Vice President Hubert Humphrey and New York senator Robert F. Kennedy. Humphrey's most looming obstacle was the Vietnam War, and he tried in vain to distance himself from the ongoing bombing of North Vietnam and Johnson's failed policies. Peaceniks, basking in the afterglow of the Summer of Love, came out in droves to support their candidate, the antiwar Kennedy, even winning him the June 5 California primary. That same night Palestinian immigrant Sirhan Sirhan assassinated Kennedy. Humphrey accepted the Democratic nomination with a black cloud looming over his head, while outside the Chicago convention, police officers beat back thousands of rampaging antiwar activists in one of the most brutal riots of the riot-happy '60s.

Republican nominee Richard Nixon kicked back and watched the Democrats self-destruct. He discussed issues only vaguely, keeping his "secret plan" to end

Tin mechanical theater. The Nixon figure soft-shoes when wound up.

Nixon rhinestone jewelry.

A homemade embroidered Nixon eagle.

In 1968, the candidates traveled in buses from campaign stop to campaign stop. Before the candidate would emerge, girls in paper dresses such as the one at left performed choreographed cheers for their candidate.

THE REPUBLICAN

IMAGE

ABOVE: This card imposes Nixon's face on Abraham Lincoln.

RIGHT: A set of Nixon bubble gum cigars.

ABOVE: A Super Spiro! jigsaw puzzle.

RIGHT: I bought these rubber hand puppets of Richard Nixon and Spiro Agnew at a Manhattan head shop.

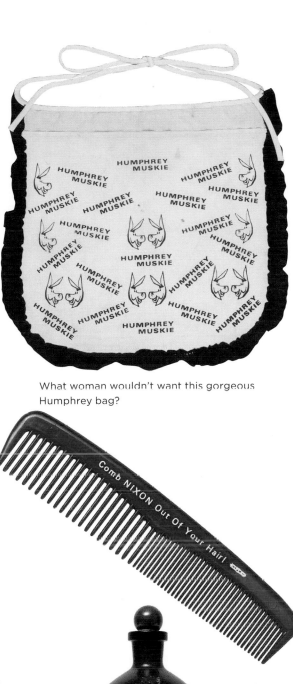

FOR A NEW DAY.
Elect
HUMPHREY!

What woman wouldn't want this gorgeous Humphrey bag?

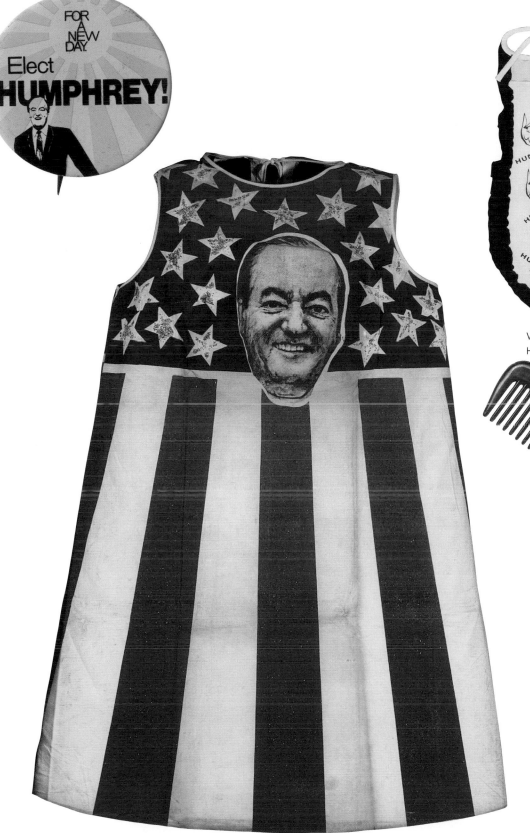

Paper dress donned by Humphrey's cheerleader.

Bank shaped like a pharmacist's bottle. Humphrey was a pharmacist before getting into politics. "Behind the times" campaign items such as this may have cost him the election.

Some talk change. Others cause it.

Humphrey

DON'T MISS IT!

ATTEND FREE! GIGANTIC! FANTASTIC!

TEXAS WANTS HUMPHREY RALLY
SUNDAY, NOVEMBER 3 - 3 P.M. - ASTRODOME
See! Hear! VICE-PRESIDENT **HUBERT HUMPHREY**
Be entertained by **FRANK SINATRA** and 40-pc. orchestra
also Nancy Sinatra, Trini Lopez, Edie Adams, The Blossoms, Flags, Patriotism, Fun!
GATES OPEN 1 PM !

TOP: Humphrey close-up poster.

BOTTOM: A poster promoting a Humphrey benefit show at the Astrodome. Can you believe that you could see the vice president, Frank Sinatra, Nancy Sinatra, Edie Adams, Trini Lopez, and the Blossoms all in one evening?

RIGHT: A Humphrey mechanical moving light box.

the war under wraps. (When asked about it after the election, Nixon admitted to having no plan whatsoever.)

Nixon opened up an early lead, but Humphrey came back strong, especially after Johnson ceased bombing North Vietnam on October 31. In the end, Nixon won the election by less than 1 percent of the popular vote. Alabama governor George Wallace, with his segregationist views, mounted a strong third-party challenge, winning forty-six electoral votes in the Deep South.

With neither Hubert Humphrey nor Richard Nixon sewing up their nominations prior to the conventions, candidates produced more materials for the primaries and state caucuses than the general election. LBJ made some items before dropping out, and Bobby Kennedy's materials included an "America Calls Another Kennedy" button featuring silhouette busts of RFK and his deceased brother. Eugene McCarthy, bitter after Kennedy beat him out as the party's primary peace candidate, produced the awkward "Kennedy is Sex, but McCarthy is Love" button (to highlight Kennedy's good looks?) as well as ideological items such as "Integrity is Alive and Well in McCarthy" and "Peace" flashers and stickers.

On the Republican side, Nixon's main adversary, Nelson Rockefeller, produced items depicting himself as a winner (and by implication, Nixon was a loser after his 1960 Kennedy defeat) with such slogans as "Rocky has Never Lost an Election" and "Go With a Winner." California governor Ronald Reagan inspired many items as well, leading to an eleventh-hour coalition combining "R & R" into a single power ticket (with the top contender left ambiguous), but the ploy fell flat.

The 1968 Nixon campaign produced boring buttons reading "Nixon," "Nixon-Agnew," or "Nixon's the One," and another ranking him alongside Washington, Lincoln, and Theodore Roosevelt. Nixon's lone Humphrey-bashing button rhythmically read "Dump the Hump." And unlike 1960, there were disappointingly no "Dick" references.

The Humphrey campaign pasted his bandannas, bubble gum cigars, necklaces, and so forth with his unfortunate initials HHH. Much more creative

Alabama governor George C. Wallace Jr. ran for president four times, as a Democrat in 1964, 1972, and 1976 and as the American Independent Party candidate in 1968, when he received 46 electoral votes.

ABOVE AND RIGHT: Robert Kennedy and Nelson Rockefeller paper dresses.

GEORGE WALLACE

RED - BLOODED AMERICAN
HONEST - CAPABLE - ENERGETIC

TEXAS DEMOCRATS FOR WALLACE

Wallace epitomized the Southern white man of the period.

items incorporated Humphrey's dad's drugstore in South Dakota (to bring out the small-town-boy vote). An old-fashioned glass medicine bottle with rounded stopper pictured the pharmacy and prescribed "HHH for Good Government." Efforts to make Humphrey appeal to the crusading liberal crowd that ferociously protested his nomination led to buttons and posters reading "Progress and Unity" and "Some Talk Change, Others Cause It."

The neo-Confederate campaign items of American Independent Party candidate George Wallace protested integration under the guise of the decline of states' rights, law and order, and neighborhood schools. His basic slogan was "Stand Up for America," and a license plate featuring a prominent Confederate flag welcomed visitors to "Wallace Country."

A breath of fresh air.

Gene McCarthy

VOTE ☒ REPUBLICAN
NIXON ★★★ AGNEW

AMERICA NEEDS WALLACE for PRESIDENT

YOUR CHOICE HUMPHREY SOCK-IT-TO-EM MUSKIE

Nemo

TOP: Bumper sticker.

ABOVE: License plate attachment.

LEFT: This button refers to Rowan & Martin's *Laugh-In* TV show.

Minnesota congressman and senator Eugene J. "Gene" McCarthy ran
unsuccessfully for the Democratic nomination in 1968 on an anti–Vietnam War
platform. He would unsuccessfully seek the presidency four more times.

VOTE REPUBLICAN ?

New York governor and businessman Nelson A. Rockefeller competed for the presidency in 1964 and 1968 as the leader of the liberal wing of the Republican Party. He later served as Ford's vice president. This photograph was taken after a group protested one of his ambitious building projects in Albany, catching Rockefeller in the act of flipping the bird to the common man.

Each sheet on the entire roll displays Nixon's name.

The new decade ushered in progressive alterations to the electoral process. First, party conventions opened their gates to an influx of women and minority delegates, and in 1971, the Twenty-sixth Amendment dropped the voting age to eighteen.

In the Democratic camp, southern states' rights champion George Wallace fought George McGovern of South Dakota during the primaries, with Wallace taking home surprising wins in Maryland and Michigan where blue-collar workers felt that the Democrats had conceded too much power to minorities. However, a gunman cut Wallace's campaign short at a Maryland rally with five swift bullets, including one in his spinal column, paralyzing the segregationist from the waist down, and handing the nomination to McGovern.

Although the Watergate burglary had already taken place, the secret was still concealed, allowing Richard Nixon and

> **Nixon was the first president to resign his office.**

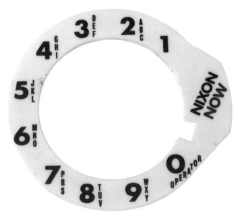

ABOVE: Nixon telephone rotary dial cover.

RIGHT: A Nixon silk banner.

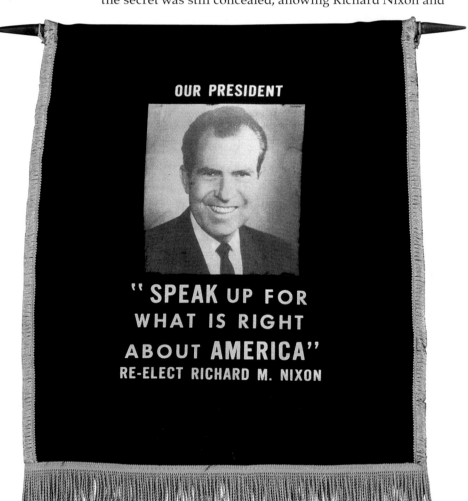

OUR PRESIDENT

" SPEAK UP FOR WHAT IS RIGHT ABOUT **AMERICA**"
RE-ELECT RICHARD M. NIXON

ABOVE, LEFT: This poster was made exclusively for Halloween.

ABOVE: Nixon cigarettes with one of his most famous expressions on the box.

LEFT: A Nixon poster including all his greatest moments.

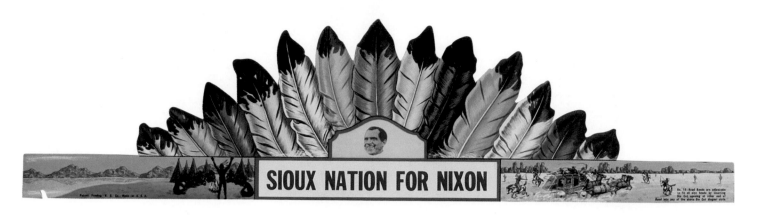

SIOUX NATION FOR NIXON

This pro-Nixon multicolor feathered headdress was perhaps the only campaign item ever to appeal exclusively to Native Americans, albeit offensively. What member of the Sioux community would actually wear this rude cowboys-and-Indians paper crown?

Spiro Agnew to win easy renomination at the Republican convention. What irked voters more was the news that McGovern's running mate, Senator Thomas Eagleton of Missouri, had once undergone electric shock therapy for depression. McGovern stood by Eagleton for a while, but eventually replaced him with former Peace Corps director Sargent Shriver.

McGovern accused Nixon of being the most corrupt president in U.S. history, but Nixon still trounced him by nearly twenty million votes.

The Vietnam War and the turbulent '60s had spawned an army of reform-minded activists, leading to hordes of rambunctious zealots vying for president in the Democratic Party or on their own. However, none of these eccentric candidates made a dent in November.

The Nixon campaign produced such odd clothing pieces as scarves and suspenders along with reelection buttons like "Four More Years" and "Nixon Now More Than Ever" in gigantic quantities due to the unprecedented amount of cash accumulated through fundraisers. Nixon's incumbency (along with his zest for being in charge) led to bumper stickers and buttons labeled simply "The President," or that exclaimed, "Right On, Mr. President" and "Young Voters for the President." Nixon used his withdrawal of most troops from Vietnam in November 1972 as passage onto the peace train. One button featured a soaring dove trumpeting, "Peace/Strength/Stability," while another read "America Anew in '72/ Nixon-Agnew for the Red, White and Blue."

Nixon aluminum-foil flag.

In Concert at the Forum-April 15th · 8:30 PM

Carole King   Barbra Streisand   James Taylor

♪ ¾ **McGovern**

Use the Power 18 Register and Vote

Quincy Jones and his Orchestra

Ushers: Warren Beatty · Jack Nicholson · Julie Christie · Sally Kellerman · James Earl Jones · Jacqueline Bisset
Michelle Gilliam · Mike Nichols · Shirley MacLaine · Goldie Hawn · Gene Hackman · Elliott Gould
Marlo Thomas · Burt Lancaster · Jon Voight · Raquel Welch · Michael Sarrazin · Britt Ekland and more

LEFT: McGovern's concerts featuring famous pop acts attempted to court young voters.

While Nixon's well-oiled fundraising machine pumped in the cash from special interest groups, the McGovern campaign's shortage on funds led to one of the most creative sets of items in years. Rising costs forced Democratic higher-ups to hand over a majority of its campaign to local fundraising efforts. Prizes to donors were reminiscent of a PBS pledge drive. Twenty-five dollar donors were awarded "McGovern Million Member Club" buttons and membership cards, while contributions of a dollar bought "Buck Nixon/I Did" buttons.

Once the donations rolled in, production began. Smiley faces and "Robin McGovern" caricatures playfully promoted their candidate. A "Gay Citizens for McGovern" button was the first of its kind in national presidential politics, and feminist group buttons replaced the o in McGovern with the ancient sign of the female. The "I Love McGov" campaign lunged at Nixon as well, with buttons reading "The Committee to Reject the President," "Nixon's Through in '72" and

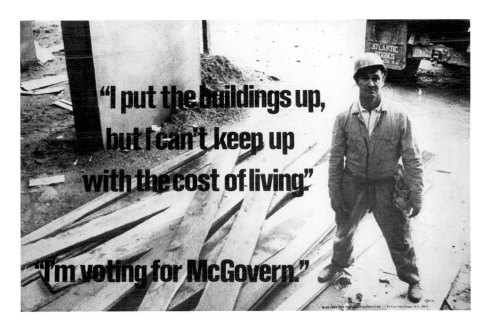

THE DEMOCRATIC PROCESS 1972

★ ★ ★ ★

McGOVERN ~~EAGLETON~~ ~~MUSKIE~~ SHRIVER

McGovern had tough luck with vice presidential nominees. First, word of Eagleton's electroshock treatments leaked. Then Senator Ed Muskie turned him down because he felt burned by the media after they claimed he was crying (which Muskie vehemently denied, claiming the snow was in his eyes). McGovern finally settled on Sargent Shriver, founder of the Peace Corps and husband of Eunice Kennedy.

"Nixon's Doing the Job of Three Men" with caricatures of the Marx brothers. Peace-loving items used Nixon's words "Those who have had a chance for four years and could not produce peace should not be given another chance" against him, with some posters carrying the full text of his self-incriminating statement.

McGovern bubble gum cigars. Promoting voting and smoking to children?

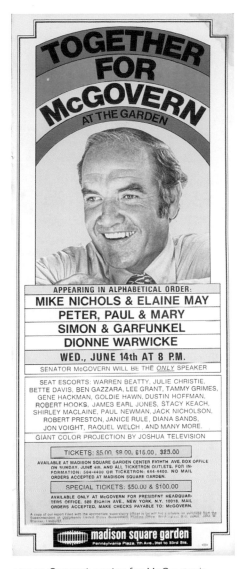

ABOVE: Concert poster for McGovern's Madison Square Garden show.

Chain necklace with McGovern pendant.

I bought this lowbrow Nixon-bashing toilet seat at a New York City head shop.

This is the first iron-on patch created as presidential memorabilia. I bought it at the McGovern Boutique, a shop devoted to McGovern set up in New York City for the six months prior to Election Day.

Windup walking peanut.

Carter was the first president born in a hospital.

With the stench of Nixon's disgrace still fresh, Democrats knew the Republicans would have a hard time hanging on to the White House, causing more than a dozen Democrats to dive brazenly into the pool. The first to get his feet wet was former Georgia governor (and peanut farmer) Jimmy Carter, who announced his candidacy in December 1974. At first, no-name Carter and his big, toothy grin didn't even show up on the national public opinion polls, leaving people saying, "Jimmy who?" But once some early primary victories rolled in, the convention handed Carter the nomination on the first ballot. Jimmy spoke of restoring people's faith in government, and his down-home personality helped distance him from the grimy Washington regulars of Nixon's inside jobs.

Although Gerald Ford had been president for over a year, former California governor Ronald Reagan put his nomination in jeopardy. Reagan ran strongly in the primaries, but Ford held him off at the convention, taking the nomination with 1,187 votes to Reagan's 1,070.

Early polls showed Carter leading Ford by more than thirty percentage points, but as the debates neared, the president narrowed the gap. However, Ford probably lost the race during the second debate, when he said, "There is no Soviet domination of Eastern Europe and there never will be under a Ford Administration." How about Poland, Mr. President?

The November election attracted one of the lowest turnouts of the century, with toothy Carter barely beating out the president. Carter's victory made him the first president elected from the Deep South since Zachary Taylor in 1848.

In an interview with *Playboy* magazine, Carter admitted to having "lusted in his heart" for many years for many women. The Republicans loved it, and released a heart-shaped button, and incorporated Goldwater's still famous slogan into the parody, "In His Heart, He Knows Your Wife." Carter's gaffes and idiosyncrasies made 1976 one of the funniest for campaign items.

During his battle to retain the presidency, Ford's boring buttons read simply "President Ford '76" or "He is Making Us Proud Again," desperately trying to distance himself from Nixon and somehow trick the public into forgetting his premature Nixon pardon. Other buttons focused on Ford's wife, Betty, who in many circles was more popular than the president.

ABOVE: This can for coins used Carter's coincidental initials (J.C.) to portray him as a Christ-like figure. Assuming that Christians would find this insufferably offensive, to whom does this item appeal?

RIGHT: Plastic peanut bank sporting "the grin."

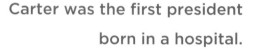

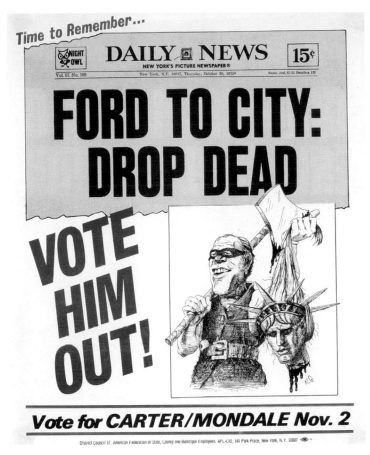

However, most Republican regalia took swings at Carter. His indecisiveness on issues prompted the Ford campaign to refer to plaid as "Jimmy Carter's Favorite Color." His toothy grin led to buttons reading "Carter Hasn't Shown Me Anything but His Teeth." Most of the satiric Ford buttons poked fun at Carter's use of the peanut as his primary campaign symbol. One button style depicted GOP elephants eating or stomping on peanuts and saying "Let's Crush Carter's Nut!" Others read "Don't Settle for Peanuts" and "Carter's Brain is the Size of A Peanut." In the end, however, the humorous jabs at Carter probably hurt Ford's chances. Belittling Carter didn't sit well with the still-angry public, especially when they associated Ford with Nixon and questioned his recent pardoning.

With the Democrats having a very legitimate shot at the presidency, they didn't skimp on Carter's campaign, in hopes that "The Grin Will Win." Playing on Carter's "Good Ole Boy" charm, the campaign referenced his hometown of Plains, Georgia, and called him "A Man of the Soil," dressing him in a weather-beaten denim workshirt for some posters. They made odd items such as luggage tags, mirrors, and plastic whistles. But the most useless and tacky items of all featured Carter's home state's favorite export, the Georgia peanut. They made peanut cuff links, peanut earrings, peanut-shaped belt buckles, peanut lapel pins—some of which incorporated real peanuts! Buttons read "Peanut Power," "I Work for Peanuts," "I am Nuts about Carter," and "I am Your Peanut Pal."

Items against Ford focused on the preemptive pardon with "Vote For Carter/Ford Will Pardon You," "Pardon Me Gerald," and "I Beg Your Pardon" buttons, along with a button proclaiming Ford as "Nixon's Choice."

With New York City going bankrupt, Mayor Abraham Beame appealed to President Ford for help. Ford claimed that bailing out the city was not the responsibility of the federal government. The *New York Daily News* blew Ford's modest rebuff out of proportion with an outlandish headline (Ford never told the city to "drop dead") and an unsettling caricature of the president wearing an executioner's mask, holding the disembodied head of Lady Liberty.

Lest we forget...

PROTEST!
GOP CONVENTION   AUG 15-19
KANSAS CITY
Penn Valley Park Kemper Arena

FOR MORE INFORMATION, CALL 816-931-3371 (KANSAS CITY) or 212-533-5028 (NEW YORK)
or write: YIPPIE, 3938 Harrison St., Kansas City, Mo.

RIGHT: This picture was taken as Ford was about to accept the nomination to be Nixon's new vice president, and used by Democrats to portray Ford canoodling with the bad guy.

The tight 1976 election produced fewer buttons than usual due to new fundraising limits passed as a reaction to the Watergate scandal, but many local party groups and new political action committees picked up the slack. The United Auto Workers and the National Education Association, among others, distributed mass quantities of Carter-Mondale items to their members and the public. The competition between these groups and retail outlets reaped creative results, including a rectangular Carter button with a small flashing red light powered by a hearing aid battery.

Amazingly, a pair of third parties far past their prime hung on in 1976, with the Communist ticket producing "Beat Big Business" buttons and the Prohibition Party encouraging the public to "Vote Dry."

Ford pin with a blinking red light (there is a battery on the back).

Classic Ford poster with his most famous slogan.

Ford Model T necklace. One of many items linking Ford to the automobile manufacturer.

Patriotic glasses. Photos of Ford dangle from the wearer's ears.

Interest rates soared, inflation swelled, and the Iranian hostage crisis dragged on with no end in sight. On top of all this, Carter had to face a challenge by Senator Edward Kennedy of Massachusetts in the primaries. The liberal wing of the Democratic Party rallied around the youngest of the Kennedy brothers, but not long into the race, Kennedy's past caught up to him. In 1969, Kennedy's car careened off a bridge on Chappaquiddick Island, part of Martha's Vineyard. He survived, but waited far too long to report that a female passenger in his vehicle had died in the accident. Criminal charges were never filed, but many people questioned his conduct. Kennedy lost the primary, but his campaign disrupted the party and left Carter in sorry shape for November.

Ronald Reagan, who nearly beat Gerald Ford in 1976, took the Republican nomination easily, leading one of his Republican challengers, Representative John Anderson of Illinois, to drop out and run his own third-party campaign. Anderson straddled the line between Reagan's conservative economic philosophy and Carter's commitment to social welfare.

Reagan made some passionate statements about toughening up on the Soviet Union, but on television, his natural charm and leadership shone. At one point during the televised debate, Reagan locked eyes with the camera and asked

Amy Carter (Jimmy's daughter) play set featuring cardboard likenesses of Amy, her father and mother, as well as Secret Service agents. How hilarious would it be to set up Amy's little lemonade stand outside the White House?

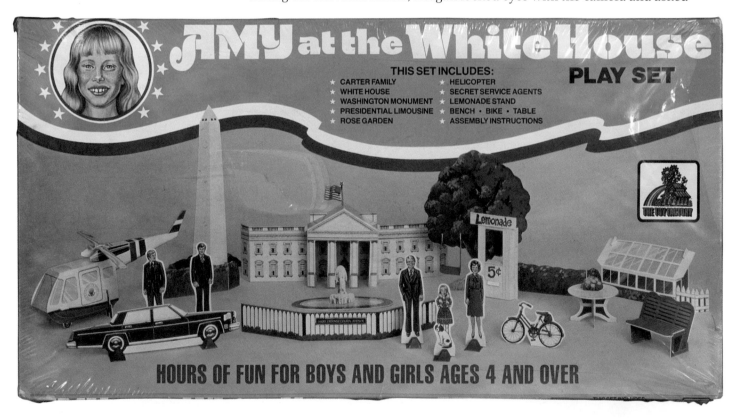

Carter "Happy Mouth" bottle opener. Notice the disturbing mono-tooth.

Bank featuring Carter atop an oversized peanut.

ABOVE: I bought this grotesque Carter/cat pillow from a woman outside the Democratic convention. I may have been her only customer.

RIGHT: Stuffed dolls of Carter and his wife, Rosalynn, with photograph faces.

The time
is now.
Reagan & Bush

A poster of Reagan and Bush in front of the podium at the Republican convention.

Reagan was the first president to have been divorced.

"Reagan" in Hebrew.

America, "Are you better off than you were four years ago?" The resounding "No" resulted in a Reagan rout.

Nineteen eighty was a ho-hum election for regalia due to Reagan's lack of thematic focus and the Carter camp's waning enthusiasm. Edward Kennedy had more campaign items for his primary bid than Carter had for his entire national campaign.

Third parties of note included the Citizen's Party ticket of Barry Commoner and LaDonna Harris (the first Native American to run for national office), who stirred up the airwaves by using the word "Bullshit" in their radio and TV ads. The John Anderson campaign was too busy haggling over ballot access, federal election funds, and access to televised debates to devote any effort toward creative trinketry.

The unsuccessful and unenthusiastic campaign to reelect Jimmy Carter was less creative (nothing to match the peanuts, grits, and grins of 1976), and produced fewer items than

GO HOME
PEANUT FARMER
THE
REAGANS
ARE COMING
1980

the earlier campaign. The Democrats marketed Carter not as the Good Ole Boy, but as a sober world statesman facing tough problems, which came across as making futile excuses for his mishaps. At least his Reagan-roasting buttons were funny, calling his rival "The Fascist Gun in the West" and imploring voters to "Send Reagan Back to Central Casting."

Although supporters of Reagan celebrated his famous conservatism, they chose not to feature it in his campaign items. Instead they settled on bright colors with upbeat slogans like "Let's Make America Great Again," "The Time is Now," and "A New Beginning" and tried to conceal Reagan's sixty-nine years of age by using retouched photographs.

A poster for John Anderson, Republican Congressman from Illinois, running as an independent.

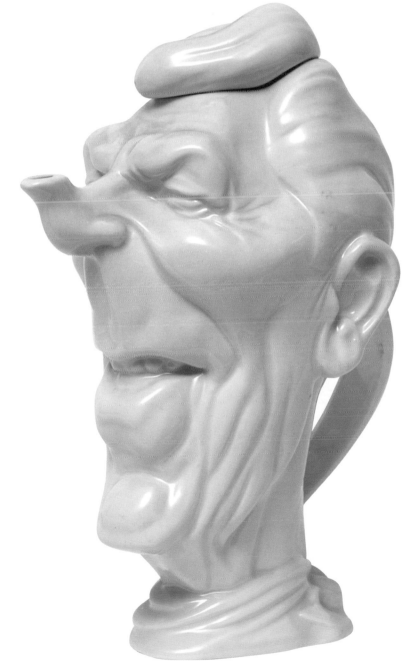

I found this Reagan teapot in England. They also sold a version featuring Margaret Thatcher.

Ted Kennedy teddy.

This Reagan jack-in-the-box has no underlying political message as far as I can tell. Perhaps he was full of surprises? Always popping up when you least expected?

Jackson 1984 for President

Jesse Jackson for President Committee
311 So. Broad St. · Phila. Pa. 19107
Phone (215) 546-3012
Authorized by Friends of Jesse Jackson for President

ABOVE: Civil rights activist and Baptist minister Jesse L. Jackson ran for the Democratic nomination in 1984 and 1988. A prominent leader of the American Christian left, he is only the second African-American to run for a national party nomination (the first being Shirley Chisolm). He is the father of Democratic congressman Jesse Jackson Jr. of Illinois.

RIGHT: Reagan's face, teddy body.

Reagan had reelection wrapped up. With the recent recession bottoming out, new hirings cutting unemployment in half, and a country at peace, he knew he had nothing to dread.

Jimmy Carter's vice president Walter Mondale led the Democratic pack, with Senator Gary Hart of Colorado and the Reverend Jesse Jackson clawing and biting behind him. Jackson was the first African-American to run a major national campaign for president, and worked to organize a "rainbow coalition" to speak for poor and disadvantaged minority voters.

Mondale won the nod and at the Democratic national convention in July, he unveiled two major surprises. First, he chose Representative Geraldine Ferraro of New York as his running mate, making Ferraro the first woman to run on a major-party ticket. Second, he brazenly declared that he would raise people's taxes to bring soaring budget deficits under control. "Mr. Reagan will raise taxes, and so will I," Mondale said. "He won't tell you. I just did." On the other hand, Reagan promised to raise them only as a last resort. He also put a new spin on his old mantra, claiming that most Americans were better off than they had been four years earlier, and few could argue. "It's morning in America . . ." Reagan's TV ads began; he won a landslide victory.

Even without any cohesive themes or symbols, Reagan dominated. Though staunchly to the right, he had won over a diverse public by sugarcoating his words just enough to win universal appeal.

The only chunk of the electorate that wasn't sold on Reagan was American women (a significant group of voters). Reagan opposed affirmative action quotas and other feminist objectives, and with a female on the opposing ticket, Republicans needed to act fast to veil their candidate's chauvinism. The result was the "Women for Reagan" campaign, producing the largest amount of women-oriented campaign items in history.

Mondale's political memorabilia, like Reagan's, lacked ideology and creativity. Reagan-bashing buttons featured such slogans as "Dump Reagan," "Pot is an Herb, Reagan is a Dope," and "Let Them Eat Jellybeans" (a play on Marie Antoinette's encouraging her subjects'

The quintessential Reagan poster.

HOPPIN' AND Poppin' FOR REAGAN '84

The Republicans had an old-fashioned popcorn machine at their convention, and delegates used these bags to scoop up their portions. It was a feat for me to find a bag devoid of buttery stains and marooned kernels.

with the President
July 27, 1987 West Bend, WI

Decal provided by Serigraph Sales & Mfg. Co., Inc., West Bend, WI 53095

Reagan distributed these boxed lunches at a speech he delivered in July 1987. Alas, I do not know what delectable treats once resided in this box.

One-of-a-kind ceramic Ray-Gun.

The time is now. Reagan Bush

REAGANOMICS BANK

ABOVE: A coin bank. The theory behind Reaganomics: By imposing fewer taxes on the rich, their spending would trickle down to the rest of society.

RIGHT: Front and back of a Reaganomics satirical doll. Supply: a smiling Reagan; demand: the poor reduced to barrel attire.

SUPPLY SIDE
REAGANOMICS D
SUPPLY SIDE

DEMAN
REAGANOMIC
DEMAND SIDE

Poster inspired by the famous "Liberty Leading the People" painting, with Ferraro in place of Lady Liberty. Histrionic?

cake consumption, and in reference to Reagan's undying love for JellyBellys), and the popular movie *Ghostbusters* inspired "Reaganbuster" buttons, but Mondale's own items stuck to run-of-the-mill red, white, and blue with banal slogans. Mondale's campaign was infamous for its wealth of items contributed by special interests such as the United Auto Workers. Though his campaign benefited from the increased funding, their endorsements led to the public perceiving him as dependent upon the unions.

Geraldine Ferraro certainly brought attention to the Mondale ticket. Chauvinists chastised the pairing; however, most items took aim at Mondale rather than his running mate. A poster read "Hurry Up, Fritz," with a caricature of Ferraro pulling puppy Mondale on a lead. Feminist memorabilia often printed Ferraro's name more prominently, or even resorted to "Ferraro and What's His Name." Poor Mondale.

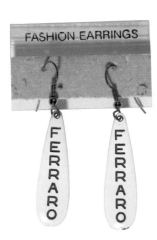

Fashionable? Ferraro earrings.

BushWackers!™
It's Good, Clean Political Paddleball Fun!

A fter eight charming years in office, Reagan endorsed his stick-in-the-mud vice president George Bush to carry his torch. Republicans knew better than to go against the popular Reagan's wishes, nominating Bush who in turn scooped up Dan Quayle for his running mate.

Senator Gary Hart of Colorado sat proudly as the Democratic frontrunner until swirling rumors of his infidelity caused him to challenge reporters to follow him. Days later reporters snapped a shot of a blonde South Carolina beauty queen cozyed up in Hart's lap on a boat called *Monkey Business*. Needless to say, he did *not* win the nomination. The Reverend Jesse Jackson did surprisingly well in the primaries, but the country wasn't quite ready for an African-American president, especially one who referred to New York City as Hymietown. So who could the Democrats turn to? The competent, uninteresting, and emotionless Massachusetts governor, Michael Dukakis.

Though taking an early lead, Dukakis's missteps doomed his campaign. Under his governorship, Massachusetts prisons ran a weekend furlough program. One murderer named Willie Horton took his vacation a bit too far. A Bush campaign item, a Monopoly-inspired Get Out of Jail Free card, reported: "Michael Dukakis's furlough plan allowed convicted murderers to take weekend leave from prison. One, Willie Horton, left and never came back. Instead he viciously raped and beat a woman while her fiancé was forced to helplessly listen to her screams. Mike Dukakis is the killer's best friend and the decent honest citizen's worst enemy." Uncompromisingly harsh, it sliced through the public perception of Dukakis's reliability and honor.

Bush Whacker paddleball set.

YOU ARE NO JACK KENNEDY VOTE DUKAKIS-BENTSEN 1988

KEEP AMERICA STRONG

VOTE DEMOCRATIC

©POLITICAL ANIMAL™

GET OUT OF JAIL, FREE

COMPLIMENTS OF MICHAEL DUKAKIS
DISTRIBUTED BY COLLEGE REPUBLICAN NATIONAL COMMITTEE
®1988 CRNC

This Monopoly-themed item reminded voters of Dukakis's leniency on jail time while he was governor of Massachusetts.

DAN QUAYLE'S MOTHER NOW BELIEVES IN ABORTION

'Bush Reminds Every Woman of Her First Husband'

This poster lampoons the "Dukakis in a tank" press nightmare.

This item pokes fun at Dukakis's exaggerated features, including his unkempt eyebrows.

Then there was the "Dukakis in a tank" blunder. Dukakis's PR people decked him out in military gear and had him ride around in a tank with his head sticking out. Intended to portray him as strong on defense, it made him look weak in the head. These events plus Dukakis's poor debate performance propelled Bush into the White House.

Bush knew that he was the heir to the most popular president since Roosevelt, and invoked Reagan when and wherever he could, with buttons urging voters to "Continue the Reagan Revolution" and sneaking Reagan's image alongside Bush and Quayle as though he was the third member of the ticket. One

Dukakis foam #1's distributed at the Democratic convention.

Dukakis's "Presidential Blend" coffee.

famous button entitled "Republican Integrity" pictured George Bush alongside Reagan, Abraham Lincoln, Theodore Roosevelt, and Dwight Eisenhower. Dukakis-demeaning buttons reminded him "Don't Mess With Texas" and another said Dukakis could do the job of three men and pictured the Three Stooges. Zing!

Though a few pins attacked Bush, including "Stop the Monster Frankenbush, Son of Reaganstein" and "If You Survived the Reagan Years – Don't Bush Your Luck," most targeted nervous nail biter and candidate least likely to win a spelling bee, Dan Quayle. A Quayle portrait included googly eyes swimming freely around his empty head, and a button read "Ornithology quiz: Which one is the birdbrain?," leaving you to choose between pictures of Quayle and a real bird.

Most of the Dukakis-Bentsen stock pictured the candidates with "1988" scrawled above them, but were so adventuresome as to add a photo of the White House. "Democratic Integrity" countered its Republican version picturing Dukakis beside Thomas Jefferson, Andrew Jackson, Franklin Roosevelt, Harry Truman, and John Kennedy. A number of items referred to Dukakis as "Duke," including a "We're With the Duke" button, though these items lacked forethought. A Louisiana-based white supremacist also ran for the presidency in '88. His name? David Duke.

A handheld boxing Bush.

Cigarettes distributed at the Republican convention. In 1988, smoking may not have been quite as taboo as today, but it was still suprising that the Republicans would promote it.

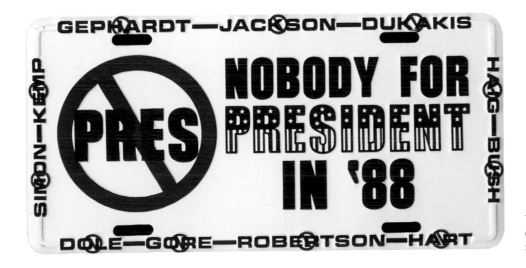

This real bush is almost twenty years old now and fading fast, as you can see. Should I replace it? Water it?

H. Ross Perot, the billionaire businessman from Texas, is best known as the Reform Party candidate for president in 1992 and 1996. In 1992, Perot ran with retired vice admiral James Stockdale, a former Vietnam POW. At one point Perot led the polls with 39 percent, and garnered 18.9 percent of the vote on Election Day, making him the most successful independent candidate in terms of the popular vote since Theodore Roosevelt in 1912. Perot's portion dipped to a paltry yet respectable 8 percent of the popular vote in 1996.

Americans wanted change. With the economy slipping and the political parties bickering, the climate called for a new kind of politician, and H. Ross Perot fit snugly into the shoes. Perot broke onto the political scene with the renegade zest of a shoot-'em-up outlaw and the deep pockets of a Texas billionaire. He poured millions into his campaign, and by the end of the primaries, Perot sat grinning big ear to big ear, equal in the polls with his two party-affiliated opponents.

Following the swift Gulf War, President Bush rode a wave of high approval, which caused many Democratic higher-ups to see the 1992 presidential race as unwinnable. This opened the door for upstart William Jefferson Clinton. Rumors of adultery and avoidance of military service threatened to end Clinton's effort prematurely, but the dapper Clinton laughed off the accusations as "a draft

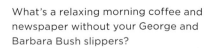

What's a relaxing morning coffee and newspaper without your George and Barbara Bush slippers?

I never dodged and a woman I never slept with," and the "Comeback Kid," as he coined himself, earned the Democratic nod.

In spite of his strong early showing, Perot dropped out of the race in July, leaving Bush and Clinton to fight it out. By the time of the election, Bush had successfully steered the sluggish economy into the basement, and in a desperate attempt to reverse the damage, reneged on his famous claim, "Read my lips, no new taxes," which Democrats relished in pointing out. Conversely, Clinton promised welfare and economic reform, and presented himself as a centrist New Democrat.

Then to the surprise of the nation, high-roller Ross returned for vengeance in October, spending an estimated $2,000,000 a day during the final month of the campaign, easily trumping the other two candidates' combined totals. In the end, Ross amassed 19 percent of the popular vote but a fat goose egg in the electoral column in a Clinton victory.

Perot racked up the most votes of any independent since Teddy Roosevelt's Bull Moose effort in 1912, mostly due to the exorbitant sums he tossed at advertising. His materials played on his immense wealth and savvy business skills and declared "Ross for Boss," not for president, a subtle nuance of his antipolitical campaign. Others included patriotic eagles and Uncle Sams, as well as the

A metalsmith–fellow collector from Pennsylvania made this anti-Clinton bank that spits coins into the Treasury as a prototype and sent it to me. "Do you want to go in together and sell these?" "Not really," I replied, "but I'll buy this one off you," making this a one-of-a-kind item.

Perot capitalized on the popularity of troll dolls in 1992. Notice the ear similarities.

This rubber waffle satirized Clinton's reputation for changing his mind on the issues. Syrup?

campaign slogan he lifted from the movie *Network* which he would speak in his Texas squeak, "I am mad as hell and I am not going to take it anymore."

Bush's items dwelled ceaselessly on his Desert Storm victory, imploring voters to "Re-Elect Our Desert Storm Commander in Chief" and "Don't Change the Team in the Middle of the Stream." The Republicans made the campaign a family affair with posters and buttons displaying Mrs. Bush and Mrs. Quayle as well as the Bush family dog, Millie. Anything to keep attention away from the economy.

Barbs on Clinton took jibes at his denial of smoking pot with the clever "Inhale to the Chief," but most referenced his supposedly scandalous lifestyle with a "Clinton after Dark—His Life in The Fast Lane: Fast Music, Fast Women and Fast Food" pin as well as "Another Nymphomaniac for Clinton." These items just made it all the more clear that Clinton, age forty-six, was cool, and Bush, sixty-eight, was a total square.

Instead of downplaying his quasihipness, Democrats embraced Clinton's cool, making his saxophone a major focus of their effort with slogans including "Clinton: A Cure for the Blues" and "Blow Bill Blow," along with a button picturing Aretha Franklin, Elton John, Barbra Streisand, Fleetwood Mac, and Bill Clinton in sunglasses blowing his horn. Another button showed President

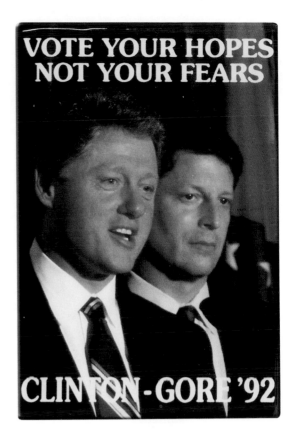

Truman holding up the famous *Chicago Tribune* newspaper, with the headline changed to "Clinton Beats Bush." Clinton's campaign created memorabilia for controversial groups, including gays and lesbians, Haitians, proponents of affirmative action, pro-choice advocates, and even button collectors. And while Bush bashed Clinton for acting like a rebellious teen, Clinton called Bush out as a liar and a nerd, with items inscribed "Bush: Bombs, Bullets and Bullshit" and "Bush Reminds Every Woman of Her First Husband." But the Democrats pulled out all the stops insulting Quayle, with pins ranging from funny to unabashedly offensive, including "Dan Quayle's Mother Now Believes in Abortion" and "Elect the Underachievers in '92," picturing Quayle and Bart Simpson.

A limited-edition button designed by the artist Roy Lichtenstein.

These were some of the first buttons produced by the Clinton campaign. The slogans mean "Friend of Bill" and "Friend of Hillary."

Clinton could sit back in his big Oval Office easy chair. He had rescued the economy from the doldrums, and the lack of imminent foreign threats had kept his weak foreign policy skills under wraps. To challenge him, the Republicans nominated aging Senator Bob Dole of Kansas, who trumped uber-conservative Pat Buchanan in the primaries.

The Clinton campaign tried to pigeonhole Dole as a past-his-prime conservative out of touch with the mainstream, and rickety Dole inadvertently helped out at every turn. Dole fell off the stage during a campaign event, and in September made reference to a no-hitter thrown the day before by the

By electing him, Bill Clinton argued that America would get two presidents for the price of one. Hillary was a policymaker in her own right.

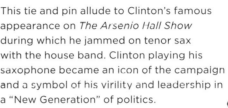

PRESIDENT CLINTON

HE BLEW
&
HE BLEW
&
HE BLEW
THEM AWAY

This tie and pin allude to Clinton's famous appearance on *The Arsenio Hall Show* during which he jammed on tenor sax with the house band. Clinton playing his saxophone became an icon of the campaign and a symbol of his virility and leadership in a "New Generation" of politics.

Limited-edition Clinton marionette.

Clinton Gore

Clinton Gore

Clinton Gore

Aldas Forever Soap

... the return of elegance.™
The design stays until the soap is gone.
Net Wt 8.5 ozs.
Red Oak Hill Inc. P.O. Box 55584 Little Rock, AR 72214

CLINTON COLA
ONE TASTE TO COME BACK 4 MORE

ABOVE: In the tradition of "Gold Water" and "Johnson Juice" comes . . . Clinton Cola!

LEFT: I bought this perfumed soap at Union Station in Washington, D.C. Supposedly, the moniker doesn't wash off (a likely story).

★ *PRESIDENTIAL TIES: NECK AND NECK FROM JEFFERSON TO CLINTON* ★
Match the tie with the President! See back for answers.

1 2 3 4 5 6

Brooklyn Dodgers, a team that had relocated to Los Angeles a mere four decades earlier. Clinton maintained a hefty lead the whole way through, even when the *Washington Post* discovered that the Democratic National Committee had received campaign contributions from Asian supporters.

Ross Perot's United States Reform Party nominated their founder, Ross Perot, but the zippy little Texan didn't stand a chance this time around, his weak polling keeping him out of the presidential debates, and Clinton clinched term number two.

What's the deal with Kansans and their sunflower? Alf Landon smacked his home state's flower on the bulk of his campaign materials in 1936, and Dole followed suit in 1996. The other campaign items made more sense, but were as dull as the Dole they supported. Materials questioning Clinton's ethics, such as "Character Matters Vote Bob Dole" items, made Dole come off like an old-timer shaking a cranky finger at a troublesome whippersnapper. In answer to Bill's '92 nickname "The Comeback Kid," Dole lamely christened himself "The Comeback Adult." One Clinton button pictured Dole smiling widely with supposed contemporary, Abe Lincoln.

The Democratic campaign's major slogans, "Building a Bridge to the Twenty-first Century" and "Clinton-Gore for the Next Generation," accentuated their

Dole's ads implied that Clinton was not to be trusted.

This plastic football referenced vice presidential nominee Jack Kemp's quarterbacking career, most notably with the Buffalo Bills, whom he led to the AFL Championship in 1964 and 1965.

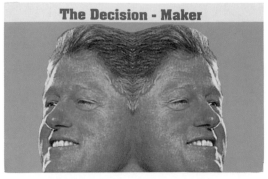

This "two-sided" Clinton poster may reference his penchant for triangulation: his ability to make the opposing side of an issue his own.

A Monopoly-style game inspired by Clinton's scandals.

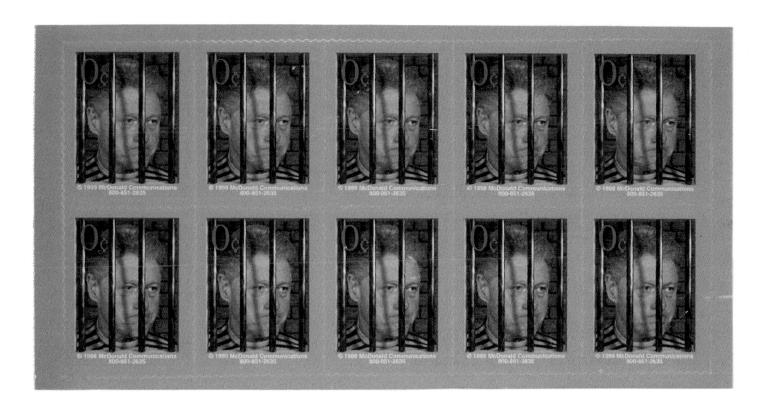

candidates' relative youth. The Democrats touted Clinton and Gore as "The Real Blues Brothers," and decked them out in Belushi and Ackroyd dark sunglasses and black suits. Other Clinton regalia included items celebrating him as the "environmental president" and my personal favorite, an "I Collect Clinton Items" button.

As they had four years earlier, Clinton and Gore hit the road with their wives on a round-the-nation bus trip titled the 21st Century Express Whistle Stop Tour. The ho-hum bus putt-putted around and communities would produce memorabilia to commemorate the visit.

This doll came equipped with suction cups to make it appear as though Clinton hung himself from your car window.

This two-headed Clinton and Dole doll makes one wonder . . . what if?

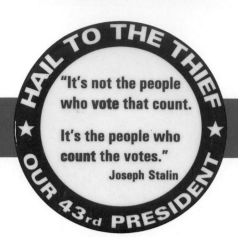

"It's not the people who vote that count.

It's the people who count the votes."
Joseph Stalin

HAIL TO THE THIEF
OUR 43rd PRESIDENT

Re-Elect 2004
Gore Lieberman

T he Bushes were back in town. Only eight years after Bush the elder left office, Republican higher-ups favored his son, George W. Bush, for president. Bush faced a small primary challenge from campaign reform crusader John McCain, but as the governor of the second largest state in the Union and favorite of the Christian right, W took the nomination easily.

Clinton's vice president Al Gore and Joe Lieberman scored the Democratic nods. Instead of trumpeting his affiliation to the two-term president, Gore avoided his former boss like the plague. Morality became a huge issue during the campaign, and many Republicans targeted licentious Clinton as the epicenter of society's ethical decay. While Bush promised to restore moral integrity with family-friendly stances on secularism, homosexuality, and abortion, Gore backpedaled over Clinton's record and his party's platform, appearing constantly stoic and robotic.

On Election Night, the race was too close to call, and balloting mistakes in Florida led to an arduous recount. The Supreme Court ended the chaos a month later in a five-to-four decision handing Bush Florida's electoral votes and, in turn, the presidency. Some fuming Democrats blamed extreme left candidate Ralph Nader, who took home a relatively quiet 3 percent of the vote, for spoiling Gore's

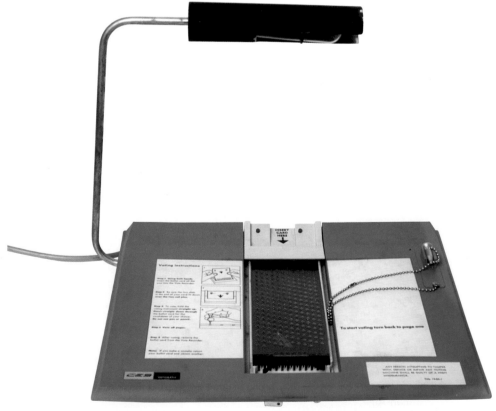

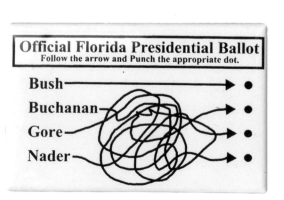

Official Florida Presidential Ballot
Follow the arrow and Punch the appropriate dot.

Bush
Buchanan
Gore
Nader

The disputed votes from Florida's Broward County inspired this ballot parody. Here is also one of the actual voting machines used on Election Day, 2000. Too difficult? Unclear? You decide.

This New York State Council of Black
Elected Democrats poster encouraged
the African-American vote.

ALL PURPOSE POLITICAL BUTTON

2000

ABOLISH: Corporate Crime, Death Penalty, Nukes & All Weapons, CIA, FBI, SOA, WTO, IMF
SUPPORT: Diversity, Feminism, NAACP, IPPN, Cooperative Community Economics, Decentralization Grassroots Democracy, People of Color

RALPH NADER for PRESIDENT

ADVOCATE: Nonviolence, Health Care for All, Animal Rights, Gun Control, Solar Energy, Green Party, Choice Voting (Proportional Representation and IRV)
END: Draft Registration, Police Brutality, Tobacco Subsidies, Hunting, Pollution, Profiteering
FREE: D.C., Puerto Rico; Mumia; Leonard Peltier, Lori Berenson, and All Political Prisoners

Liberal activist Ralph Nader ran for president four times: 1992, 1996, 2000, and 2004 (in 1996 and 2000 as the nominee of the Green Party and in 2004 as an independent). The solipsistic overabundance of text on this button may indicate why Nader did not prove victorious.

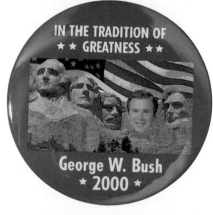

Gore's choice of Democratic senator Joe Lieberman of Connecticut as his 2000 running mate (making Lieberman the first Jewish candidate on a national ticket) inspired this yarmulke.

chances. Gore was the third candidate in U.S. history (see 1876 and 1888) to win a majority of the popular vote but still lose the race.

Mostly to distinguish him from his dad, many items referred to George Bush as "W" or spelled the phonetically classy way, "Dubya." The Bush campaign items centered on a morality theme, "Restoring Integrity," and an educational theme, "No Child Left Behind," but the most popular referred to W as a "Compassionate Conservative." Non-issue items included pins comparing W and his dad to the only other presidential father-son combo, John and John Quincy Adams. The Bush campaign also attempted to rope him in with "The Great Republican Tradition," the most laughable example being a pin superimposing Bush on Mount Rushmore. Bush-loving brigades of Christians, Jews, cat and dog lovers, and NASCAR fans produced their own W memorabilia.

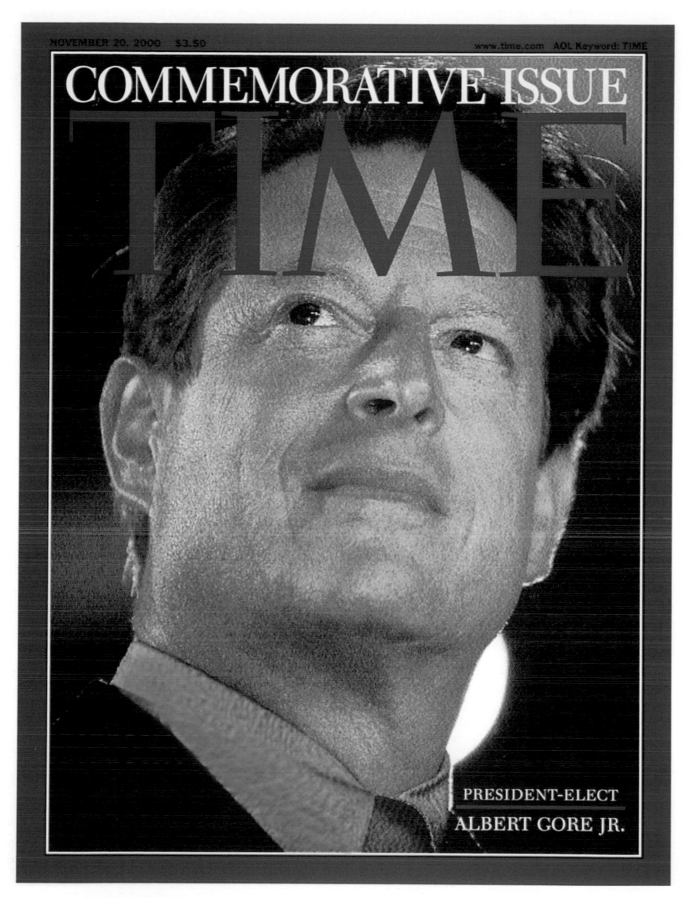

COMMEMORATIVE ISSUE

TIME

PRESIDENT-ELECT

ALBERT GORE JR.

One of five advance copies produced by
Time magazine in case the election had
ended differently.

Sore Loserman 2000

A Bush ventriloquist doll with the "Sheriff" decked out in red, white, and blue.

Bush piñata.

Bill Clinton was absent from Gore items, in attempts to disassociate Gore from Wild Bill rather than ride the incumbent's coattails, as the elder Bush had with Reagan years earlier. Instead, the Democrats focused on Gore's tree-hugging environmentalism and famous make-out session with his wife at the Democratic National Convention. Because Lieberman was the first Jew on a national ticket, many political items celebrated with pins in Hebrew, including "Chutzpah for Gore Lieberman." During the court battles following the election, Republican materials changed the Democratic ticket's name to the more appropriate "Sore Loserman 2000."

Program signed by Bill Bradley's former New York Knicks teammates. From a fundraiser at Madison Square Garden during Bradley's 2000 campaign. This was the only occasion on which the entire team came out in support of Bradley.

A witty item from the National Stone Association for the 2000 election.

Picture from Bush's famous aircraft carrier speech after the Iraq invasion.

Sending troops to Iraq runs in the family on this postcard.

George W. Bush surfed a frequently fluctuating wave of opinion during his first term in office. After September 11, the country rallied behind him. When he initiated the war on terror, the public praised him. The Iraq war, not so much. Democratic nominee Senator John Kerry of Massachusetts looked to prey on Bush's dipping popularity.

Kerry claimed that the supposedly botched war in Iraq had alienated the United States from its foreign allies and taken sorely needed forces away from the real problem, the war on terror. He wished to be "Stronger at Home, Respected in the World." Bush took this slogan as an opportunity to portray Kerry as a domestic spineless wimp.

As Kerry tried to trump up his military service in answer to Bush's allegations, his former naval friends sought to strip him of his Purple Hearts. Formed with the intention of knocking Kerry out of the race, the Swift Boat Veterans for Truth sent Kerry careening back to square one and Bush to the White House for term two.

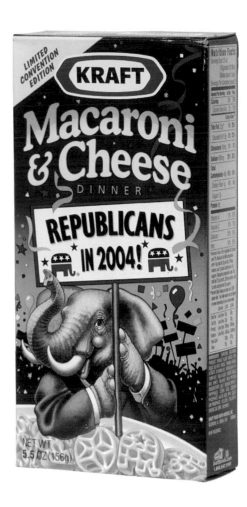

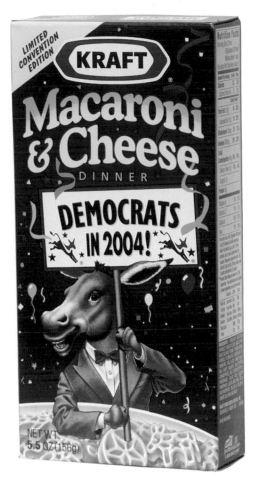

ABOVE, LEFT: John Kerry's marriage to the widow of ketchup magnate John Heinz caused Bush supporters to produce an alternative condiment. Notice the "50 states" in place of the trademark Heinz "57."

ABOVE, RIGHT: Kraft distributed these commemorative mac'n'cheeses exclusively at the party conventions. Notice there is no mention of the candidates by name.

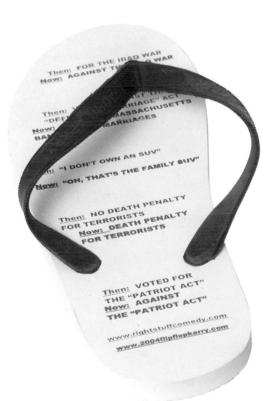

Bush's accusations of Kerry's issue "flip-flopping" in a tangible form.

Bush and Kerry inflatable punching bags.
Bush bag poised to "Knock Kerry Out."

Brother Jeb, George W., and father George. Produced in Florida where Jeb served as governor. Notice George W. is the smallest of the three.

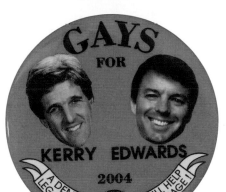

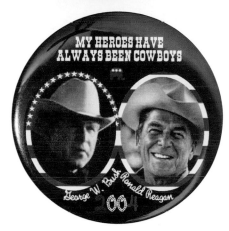

Does wearing the same hat make you the same?

Bush and Cheney give enthusiastic thumbs up as they dispose of the opposition.

Wipe your tush with this two-ply recycled toilet paper.

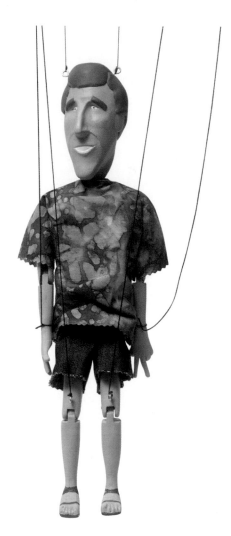

ABOVE: This Kerry marionette features the candidate in tie-dye and cutoffs, possibly in reference to his peace-loving anti-Vietnam days.

RIGHT: Hussein, Castro, and others proudly display their support for Kerry.

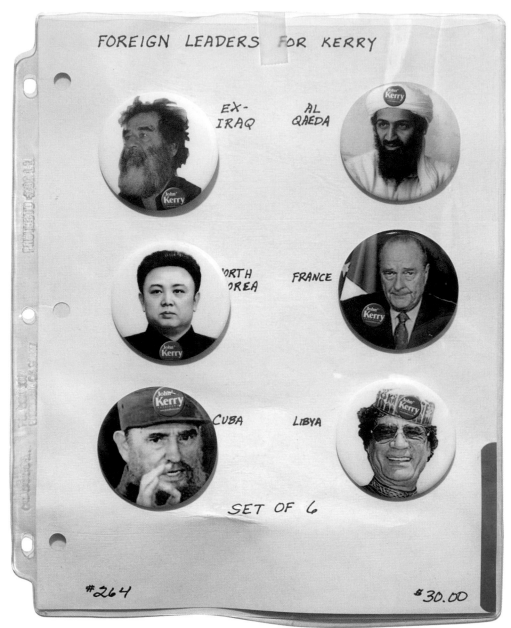

FOREIGN LEADERS FOR KERRY

EX-IRAQ

AL QAEDA

NORTH KOREA

FRANCE

CUBA

LIBYA

SET OF 6

#264

$30.00

STARS for KERRY EDWARDS

The Bush-Cheney reelection campaign focused much of its efforts on the "successful" wars in Iraq and Afghanistan, referring to the president as "America's Top Gun" on one pin, with another picturing a youthful W in Air National Guard attire touting "We Will Not Tire. We Will Not Falter. We Will Not Fail. Bush 2004." Bush's strength with the country's Christian population inspired "Christians for Bush 2004" and "Children are Gifts from God to Be Cherished, Not Aborted" items, as well as my favorite, combining church and military, "God. Guns. Guts. Bush 2004." With all this war talk, Bush needed a way to appeal to peace-minded ladies, leading to the poster, "W Stands for Women."

The Kerry campaign delved into the past, focusing a number of items not on John Kerry, but John Kennedy. Kerry capitalized on the coincidence that both men were senators from Massachusetts and shared the same initials. One button read "America Needs Another JFK" and another blatantly ripped off

VETERANS
★ AGAINST ★
JOHN KERRY

www.vietnamveteransagainstjohnkerry.com

Swift Boat scandal memorabilia.

POLITICAL PET TOYS
YOU CAN'T GET EVEN BUT YOUR PET CAN

Kerry

ABOVE: Kerry used a similar motorcycle spare tire cover on his own ride. Kerry's windsurfing, skiing, and biking during the campaign caused many voters to doubt his political passion.

LEFT: These chew toys (with squeakers) allow your pup to release its political frustrations.

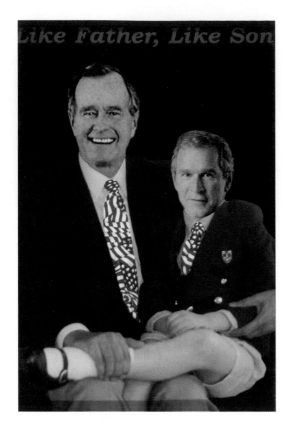

ABOVE, LEFT: This postcard superimposes a grown George W. on his father's lap. Nice calf.

ABOVE, RIGHT: Peanut butter and jelly just tastes better out of a Kerry-Edwards lunchbox.

Kennedy's 1960 slogan "All the way with JFK," but pictured John Kerry. Another of Kerry's odd campaign moves was playing up his military service in Vietnam after he'd vehemently denounced it twenty-five years earlier. "A Band of Brothers Veterans for Kerry" and "Support Our Troops Vote for Kerry" buttons amplified Kerry's indecision.

Taking jabs at Bush's alleged ignorance.

BATTLEGROUND U.S.A.

THE U.S. ELECTORAL COLLEGE PRESENTS
The Swing State Showdown
* * * November 2, 2004 * * *

THE MAIN EVENT

George W.
"Love Ya, Dubya"
BUSH
VS.
John F.
"Bring It On"
KERRY

Battling for
the title:
Leader of the
Free World

12 Rounds
No Chads
Winner Take All

PRELIMINARY BOUT - 10 ROUNDS

DICK
"You can't find me"
CHENEY
VS
JOHN
"Pretty Boy"
EDWARDS

FREE ADMISSION - JUST BE SURE TO REGISTER

(c) www.CampaignEarrings.com

Boxing poster produced by an Ohio State
University group to encourage voting.

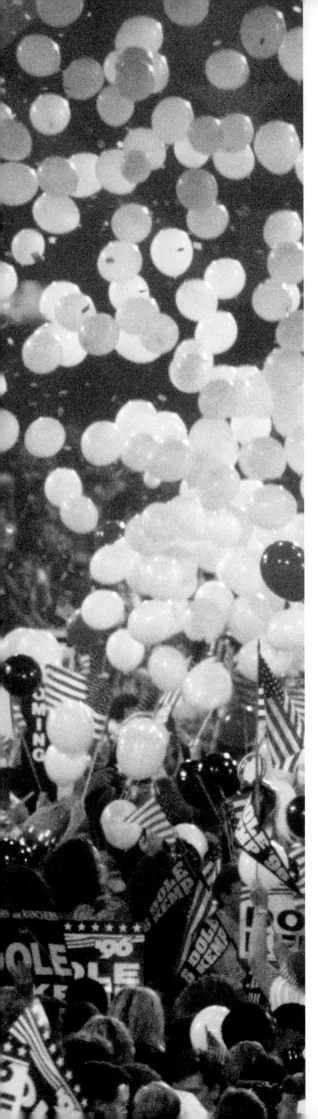

ACKNOWLEDGMENTS

Special Thanks to:

Campaigning for President: Elisabeth Dyssegaard, Jane Friedman, Phil Friedman, Patrick Gauphan, Jennifer Hintze, Jean Marie Kelly, Laura Lindgren, and Andrew Wylie.

Museum of Democracy Board of Advisors: the Honorable Michael Bloomberg, the Honorable Geraldine Ferraro, Robert F. Kennedy Jr., and the Honorable John McCain.

Museum of Democracy Board of Directors: James Cohen, Catherine Crier, Matt Gohd, Deb Gullett, Mark Halperin, Michael Jones, Daniel Mueller, Joseph Sohm, the Honorable Jay Snyder, Stuart Sundlum, Kim Taipale, and Tom Zschach.

Others: Al Anderson, Patricia Duff, Tom Healy, Fred Hochberg, Ken Hosner, the Honorable Kate Levin, and Paul Ullman.